Practical Guide to the Operational Use of the SVD Sniper Rifle

By Erik Lawrence

Copyright ©2014 Erik Lawrence

Erik Lawrence
www.vig-sec.com   erik@vig-sec.com

Although the author and publisher have made every effort to ensure the accuracy and completeness of information contained in this book, we assume no responsibility for the use or misuse of information contained in this book .errors, inaccuracies, omissions, or any inconsistency herein. Portions of this manual are excerpts from outside sources but have been validated and modified as necessary.

Printed and bound in the United States of America

First printing 2010
Second printing 2014

ISBN-10: 1-941998-08-9
ISBN-13: 978-1-941998-08-3
EBOOK – ISBN-13: 978-1-941998-27-4
LCCN: Not yet assigned

ATTENTION US MILITARY UNITS, US GOVERNMENT AGENCIES AND PROFESSIONAL ORGANIZATIONS: Quantity discounts are available on bulk purchases of this book. Special books or book excerpts can also be created to fit specific needs. For information, please contact:

Erik Lawrence
www.vig-sec.com   erik@vig-sec.com

CREDITS:
Maxim R. Popenker, Modern Firearms website, http://world.guns.ru

Wikipedia contributors, "Main Page," Wikipedia, The Free Encyclopedia,
http://en.wikipedia.org/w/index.php?title=Main_Page&oldid=83971314
(accessed October 7, 2006).

Firearms are potentially dangerous and must be handled responsibly by individuals. The technical information presented in this manual on the use of the SVD rifle reflects the author's research, beliefs, and experiences. The information in this book is presented for academic study only. Neither the author nor the publisher assumes any responsibility for the use or misuse of information contained in this book.

SAFETY NOTICE
Before starting an inspection, ensure the weapon is cleared. Do not manipulate the trigger until the weapon has been cleared of all ammunition. Inspect the chamber to ensure that it is empty and no ammunition is present. Keep the weapon oriented in a safe direction when loading and handling.

AMMUNITION NOTICE- This weapon fires the 7.62x54mm, not the 7.62x51mm NATO (.308 Winchester). Firing the incorrect ammunition will damage the weapon and possibly injure the operator.

Training should be received from knowledgeable and experienced operators on this particular weapons system. Vigilant Security Services, LLC provides this training and continually perfects its instruction with up-to-date information from actual use.

www.vig-sec.com

Table of Contents

SVD
DRAGUNOV

SNIPER
RIFLE

Section 1

Introduction

The objective of this manual is to allow the reader to be able to use the various SVD weapons competently. The manual will give the reader background/specifications of the weapon; instructions on its operation, disassembly, and assembly; proper firing procedure; and malfunction/misfire procedures. Operator-level maintenance will also be detailed to allow the reader to understand and become competent in the use and maintenance of the SVD rifle.

Description

The SVD (*Снайперская винтовка Драгунова*, pronounced *Snayperskaya Vintovka Dragunova*) is a short-stroke gas-operated weapon. When a round is fired, some of the gases that are produced from the burning of the powder enter a small gas port and push on a series of small pistons, which forces the bolt back. As the gas pressure drops, the bolt is then pushed forward by a spring. It then strips another round from the magazine and is ready to fire again.

The characteristics of the Soviet SVD Rifle:

Caliber:	7.62x54mm rimmed Russian
Operation:	Gas, semi-automatic
Capacity:	10-round detachable box magazine
Weight:	9.5 lb (4.31 kg) empty with telescope
Length:	48.2 in (122.5 cm)
Barrel Length:	24 in (62 cm)
Rifling:	4 grooves, 1:10 right-hand twist
Max Rate of Fire:	30 RPM
Aimed Rate of Fire:	6-10 RPM
Scope Type:	PSO-1 with Infrared (IR) detection capability
Scope Data:	24mm objective lens, 4x, 6 degree field of view
Maximum Effective Range:	800 Meters
Compatible Passive Night Scopes:	**NSP-3**: 2.7x, 7 degree field of view range of approx 300 yds **PGN-1**: 3.4x, 5.7 degree field of view range of 400-500 yds

Background

The SVD "Dragunov" (<u>Russian</u>: (*Снайперская винтовка Драгунова*, pronounced *Snayperskaya Vintovka Dragunova*) was designed by Jevgenyíj Fjedorovics Dragunov in the Soviet Union between 1958 and 1963. The Dragunov entered service with the Soviet army in 1963 as a main infantry sniper rifle. It replaced the Mosin Nagant bolt- action rifle. The SVD was the world's first purpose-built military precision semi-automatic marksman's rifle, and is common (along with several variants) throughout the former Eastern Bloc. The need for a new precision platoon-level, semi-automatic rifle became apparent to Soviet military leadership in the 1950s, and in 1958, a contest among Soviet arms designers was opened for the creation of such a rifle. The winner of the contest was a rifle designed by a team headed by Dragunov.

Design

The design by Dragunov was pioneered for sporting rifles and was easily adapted for military usage for the design contest.

Operation

The SVD-type rifle uses the gas-operation system to provide energy to cycle the rifle's action during the cycle of operation. In gas operation, a portion of high-pressure gas from the cartridge being fired is used to power a mechanism to extract the spent case from the chamber and load a new cartridge from the magazine to the chamber. Energy from the gas is harnessed through a port in the barrel. This high-pressure gas impinges on a surface, such as a piston head, to provide motion for unlocking of the action, extraction of the spent case, ejection, cocking of the hammer, chambering of a fresh cartridge, and locking of the action. The hammer-type trigger and firing mechanism allows it to deliver single-shot fire and to set the rifle at SAFE.

A lever-type safety is located on the right side of the receiver. The trigger mechanism detaches for cleaning or replacement. The rifle's bore and chamber are chrome-plated for ease of cleaning and resistance to corrosion.

The buttstock and hand guards are made of wood (walnut, birch, beech) or impact-resistant polymer. The wooden buttstock is furnished with a rubber butt pad for dampening recoil.

The iron sight system consists of the range-graduated leaf rear sight and an AK-type protected front sight. Both sights are adjustable for windage and elevation. The iron sight allows delivery of aimed fire with the optical sight in place. On the receiver's left side is a standard SVD rail for optical sight use. Later in the manual is a section dedicated to the optic sight systems available for the SVD-type rifle.

Variants

There are a small number of variants of the standard SVD which are listed for reference purposes.

SVD

Figure 1-1a Pre-1991 SVD

Figure 1-1b Post-1991 SVD

Caliber: 7.62x54mm

Type: Gas-operated, semi-automatic

Overall Length: 48 inches/122.5 cm

Weight Unloaded: 9.5 pounds/4.3 kg

Barrel Length: 24 inches/62 cm

Magazine Capacity: 10 rounds

Both the SVD-S and the original SVD since 1991 are produced with a polymer buttstock and magazine. The SVD also came with a bayonet identical to that of the AK-47, a cheek rest, a carrying strap, and a magazine pouch with basic cleaning/maintenance tools.

Variations with Night Vision Devices:
When the SVD has a NSPUM NVD, it is referred to as the SVDN2; when with the NSPU-3 NVD, it is referred to as the SVDN3.

SVD-S

Figure 1-2a Current SVD-S with flat-sided receiver

Figure 1-2b Early SVD-S with lightening cuts on receiver

Caliber: 7.62x54mm

Type: Gas-operated, semi-automatic

Overall Length: 44.7 inches/113.5 cm

Weight Unloaded: 10.3 pounds/4.68 kg

Barrel Length: 23.2 inches/59 cm

Magazine Capacity: 10 rounds

In 1991, the Dragunov Sniper Rifle was improved by the Izhevsk (*Izhmash*) factory. The improved sniper rifle is called the SVD-S and is intended for airborne troops. During fighting in Afghanistan, the SVD was found to be too long for carrying in helicopters and APCs. The SVD-S (*SVD - Skladnaya*) was developed for airborne and parachute troops and has a shorter barrel of 22" (565 mm). The overall length is 44.6" (1135mm), or 34.4" (875 mm) with the metal butt stock folded. The SVD-S can be fired from inside the BTR and BMP fighting vehicle from firing ports. A new 15-round magazine entered service with the SVD-S as well. It features a slightly improved and heavier barrel, a modernized receiver, a shorter barrel, and a new flash hider. For convenient handling in armored vehicles, landing craft, helicopters, and other military vehicles, the sniper rifle is equipped with a folding buttstock. The buttstock is made from metal or polymer materials and folds to the right side. The SVD-S is 21% shorter in length compared to the ordinary rifle. Other differences include: the SVD-S top cover on the receiver is made from 1mm-thick steel instead of 0.7mm as on the SVD; the gas piston diameter 9.5mm (instead of 10.5mm on the SVD); the outer barrel diameter is 1mm wider, which makes the SVD-S barrel a bit heavier; and the SVD-S muzzle brake is 2.5" (65mm) shorter.

The Izhmash arsenal changed its receiver design by eliminating the lightening cuts on the outside walls of the receivers. These military SVD-S weapons have the flat-sided receiver, the same found on US-imported commercial Tigers. This change updated the design, which adds strength to the receiver and allows it to be chambered in higher-powered calibers.

Provided in the set are:
- Magazines
- Optical sight PSO-IM2 with SPTA
- Knife-bayonet
- Rifle sling
- Accessories for cleaning and oiling
- Oiler

Variations with Night Vision Devices:
When the SVD-S has a NSPUM NVD, it is referred to as the SVDSN2; when with the NSPU-3 NVD, it is referred to as the SVDSN3.

SVD-K

Figure 1-3 SVD-K

Caliber: 9.3x64mm (compares to the .35 Whelan)

Type: Gas-operated, semi-automatic

Overall Length: 49 inches/125 cm

Weight Unloaded: 14.3 pounds/6.5 kg (empty magazine and no scope or bipod)

Barrel Length: 24 inches/62 cm

Magazine Capacity: 10 rounds

The Dragunov SVD-K is a sniper rifle produced by the former Soviet Union. It is chambered to fire 9.3mm ammunition.

The rifle features a bipod, detachable 10-round magazine, and folding stock. The rifle can accommodate any type of sighting devices for both daytime and night vision. The SVD-K entered service with Spetsnaz troops in June 2001, with the new 9.3x64 mm FMJ 9SN round (17.4 grams/268 grains at 760 meters per second/2,490 feet per second).

Tigr (Tiger)

Figure 1-4a TIGR "*THrP*" (Tiger) caliber 7.62x54mm with wood furniture

Figure 1-4b TIGR "*THrP*" (Tiger) caliber 7.62x54mm with folding buttstock

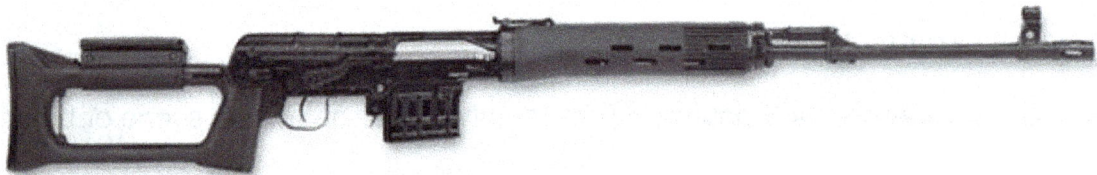

Figure 1-4c TIGR "*THrP*" (Tiger) caliber 7.62x54mm with polymer fixed buttstock

Figure 1-4d TIGR - 308 "*THrP*" (Tiger) caliber 7.62x51mm (.308 Winchester)

Figure 1-4e TIGR - 9 "*THrP*" (Tiger) caliber 9.3x64mm

Caliber: 7.62x54mm, 7.62x51mm, and 9.3x64mm

Type: Gas-operated, semi-automatic

Overall Length: See chart below

Weight Unloaded: See chart below

Barrel Length: See chart below

Magazine Capacity: 10 rounds

An SVD modification "*Tigr*" (*Tiger*) was developed for civilian and commercial use. It has a bit shorter barrel (530 mm/20.9" instead of 620 mm/24.4"). "*Tigr's*" design is similar to the SVD. The rifles are based on the venerable SVD Dragunov sniper rifle and differ in their improved accuracy of fire. The 620 mm/24.4" barrel can be special ordered from the factory on these models.

Specifications of Rifles

	"Tigr"	"Tigr-308"	"Tigr-9"
Caliber, mm	7.62	7.62	9
Cartridge	7.62x54R	.308 Win(7.62x51)	9.3x64
Barrel length, inches/mm	20.9/530	22.2/565	22.2/565
Rifle total length, mm	1100...1200	1100...1200	1100...1200
Rifle weight, empty magazine, lb/kg	8.6/3.9	8.7/3.95	8.7/3.95
Magazine capacity, rds.	5 or 10	10	5

Variations in the *Tigr*

Versions of the butt design:
- Skeleton wooden butt with a thumbhole
- Straight hunting butt
- Polymer butt- To make firing through the optical sight more comfortable, the adjustable cheek is provided
- Pistol grip and tubular metal butt folds to the right. The butt is equipped with an adjustable cheek to make firing through the optical sight more comfortable. The length of the rifle with the folded butt is reduced by 260 mm/10.2".

Versions of the hand-guard design:
- Wooden hunting
- Polymer

Versions of the front-sight base design:
- With long cylindrical flash suppressor
- With short taper flash suppressor or without flash suppressor

SVU type Bullpups

Figure 1-5a SVU Bullpup, 1975 – semi-automatic

Figure 1-5b SVU-A Bullpup, 1991 – semi- and full-automatic capable

Caliber: 7.62x54mm

Types:
- SVU - Gas-operated, semi-automatic
- SVU-A - Gas-operated - semi-automatic and full-automatic

Overall Length: 34.3 inches/87 cm

Weight Unloaded: 7.9 pounds/3.6 kg

Barrel Length: 20.5 inches/52 cm

Magazine Capacity: 10 rounds, standard issue SVD

The SVU (*Snaiperskaya Vintovka Ukorochennaya)* and SVU-A (*Snaiperskaya Vintovka Ukorochennaya - Avtomat*) Sniper Rifle Short - Automatic are used by Russian Spetsnaz teams and have the option of fully automatic fire. The semi-automatic SVU is used by Interior Ministry and OMON troops. Tula arsenal was tasked in 1975 with modernizing the SVD system and developed this model with Airborne/Special Operations troop usage in mind. Derogation in muzzle velocity and accuracy were acceptable to allow for the system to become more compact. The SVD mechanical sights were replaced with a more convenient/modern design.

And the PSO-type optical sight was utilized, but commercial optical sights could also be utilized through the use of a standard dovetail mount.

A three-chambered muzzle device was also added to the barrel-
- Muzzle Brake - designed to absorb recoil energy.
- Equalizer - designed to reduce fluctuations of the barrel.
- Balance - designed to displace the forward center of gravity of the weapon.
- Sound Suppressor - designed to control the expansion and cooling of gases inside baffle chambers, the device also reduced the level of sound from a shot.

NDM-86, Norinco, Chinese

Figure 1-6a Chinese NDM-86 (right side)

Figure 1-6b Chinese NDM-86 (left side)

Figure 1-6c Chinese NDM-86 .308 magazine and Russian SVD magazine on right for comparison

Caliber: 7.62x51mm, imported in US, commercial export

Type: Gas-operated, semi-automatic

Overall Length: 48 inches/122 cm

Weight Unloaded: 8.2 pounds/3.8 kg

Barrel Length: 24 inches/62 cm

Magazine Capacity: 10 rounds

M76 Zastava

Figure 1-7 M76 Zastava

Caliber: 7.92x57 Mauser; 7.62x51mm and 7.62x54R

Type: Gas-operated, semi-automatic

Overall Length: 44.5 inches/113 cm

Weight Unloaded: 9.3 pounds/4.2 kg

Barrel Length: 21.7 inches/55 cm

Magazine Capacity: 10 rounds

The M76 sniper rifle was developed in the late 1970s at the Crvena Zastava Arms factory in former Yugoslavia. It is still offered by the successor of Crvena Zastava, the Zastava Arms factory in Serbia. The M76 is based on the famous Kalashnikov AK action, stretched and strengthened to accept much longer and more powerful rifle ammunition. The trigger also has been limited to semi-automatic fire only. All controls and layout of the rifle are similar to the AK, and it is fitted with the typical side-rail on the left wall of the receiver, which can accept mounts for day and night scopes. The standard sight is the 4x daylight telescope, and the M76 is fitted with adjustable open sights as a back-up measure. It has a long barrel if fitted with a flash hider.

Type-79, Chinese 79式狙击步枪

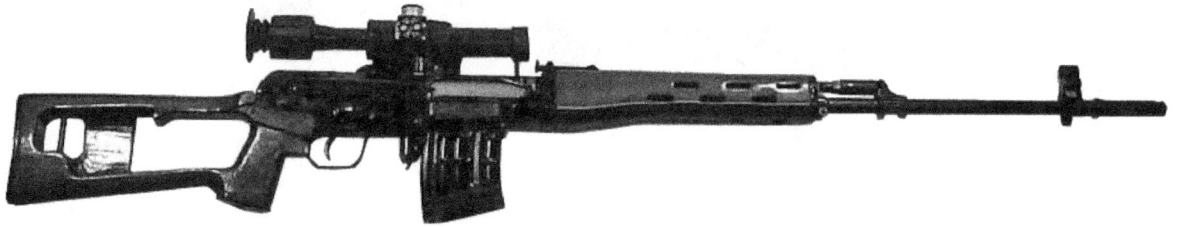

Figure 1-8 Chinese Type-79

Caliber: 7.62x54mm

Type: Gas-operated, semi-automatic

Overall Length: 48 inches/122 cm

Weight Unloaded: 8.4 pounds/3.8 kg

Barrel Length: 24.4 inches/62 cm

Magazine Capacity: 10 rounds

The NORINCO 7.62x54mm Type 79 is a precise copy of the Soviet/RFAS SVD Dragunov sniper rifle, except that the butt is slightly shorter. It is equipped with a 4x magnification optical sight that is a copy of the Soviet/RFAS PSO-1 and has the same ability to detect infra-red emissions.

Type-85, Chinese 85式狙击步枪

Figure 1-9 Chinese Type-85

Caliber: 7.62x54mm

Improved Type 79 rifle; more data in future revisions.

Type-88, Chinese 88式5.8毫米狙击步枪

Figure 1-10a Chinese Type-88

Figure 1-10b Chinese Type-88 compared to Steyr SSG

Caliber: 5.8x42mm

Improved Type 85 rifle; more data in future revisions.

Commonly Mistaken for SVD-Type Rifles

PSL, Romanian

Figure 1-11 Romanian PSL Rifle

Caliber: 7.62x54mm

Type: Gas-operated, semi-automatic

Overall Length: 46 inches/115 cm

Weight Unloaded: 8.8 pounds/4 kg

Barrel Length: 24.4 inches/62 cm

Magazine Capacity: 10 rounds

PSL (Romanian: *Puşcă Semiautomată cu Lunetă*, "scoped semi-automatic rifle")
is often confused with the SVD, but this rifle is made from the Kalashnikov
design, not the Dragunov. PSL rifles were originally made at the *Regia Autonomă
pentru Producţia de Tehnică Militară* - RATMIL Cugir arsenal in Cugir, Romania.
After a consolidation of military arsenals when Romania joined NATO, production
of the PSL is now at the SC *Fabrica de Arme Cugir* SA (ARMS arsenal) in Cugir,
Romania which is completely retooled with all brand-new, state-of-the-art modern
equipment purchased from Belgium and Croatia. Its appearance is *similar* to the
Dragunov sniper rifle, though not one single part interchanges between the rifles.

True military PSL rifles are rare in the US, and most are imported under the
model names ROMAK 3, PSL-54C, FPK, FRK Dragunov, or SSG-97
(*scharfschutzengewehr* – 1997). The military versions have the prohibited third
axis hole drilled through the receiver. A rifle with this third hole is classified as a
machinegun under ATF NFA regulations, regardless of the internal parts needed
for full-automatic fire.

Optical Sight

The current military issue POSP (PSO) series is modified for 2xLR44 (or 1xCR1/3N) 3V batteries. Compact and solidly built, the scope has a magnesium alloy body, which is finished in a "military" dark-grey protective coating. The reticules are illuminated in red, making the contrasting reticule line free of glow, which allows it to be used in dusk conditions. All three models are nitrogen-filled to prevent lens fogging, and waterproof, and come with 1000m range-finding reticules.

PSO-SERIES: All featured variants below are manufactured to meet stringent Russian military specifications and requirements, are nitrogen filled, and have fully coated high- quality lens systems. Although used in daylight without special consideration, they are also equipped with illuminated range-finding reticle systems; which allow effective targeting in low light or total darkness. Illumination units are modern, reliable, solid-state LED devices that operate on common, inexpensive batteries.

NOTE: All models shown below are available with either SVD- or AK- (V-suffix) type mounting clamps. Please specify when ordering the type and caliber of rifle you will be utilizing, as well as any other details that may help us ensure you receive the very best service. Many units are equipped with an adjustable eyepiece diopter focus (D-suffix). Standard PSO-1 series models have a fixed or omni-focus design.

All POSPs have the same minute of angle (MOA) adjustments, which is 10cm at 100 meters (or 1m at 1000m). Range finding works by placing the target (1.5m - 1.8m = 5' - 5'11" -- average human height or 0.5m -- machine-gunner) between the horizontal and the top reclining line with numbers. On the reclining line, locate the number closest to the point where the target touches the line and multiple that by 100, and this calculation will give you the distance to the target in meters (1 meter = 1.11 yards). Aiming chevrons are designed to adjust for bullet drop (when the upper mark is zeroed for 1000m) at 1100 and 1200 meters, aiming with second and third chevrons accordingly (POSP 4x24M) or (when upper mark is zeroed for 900m) at 1000, 1100, 1200, and 1300 meters (POSP 8X42).

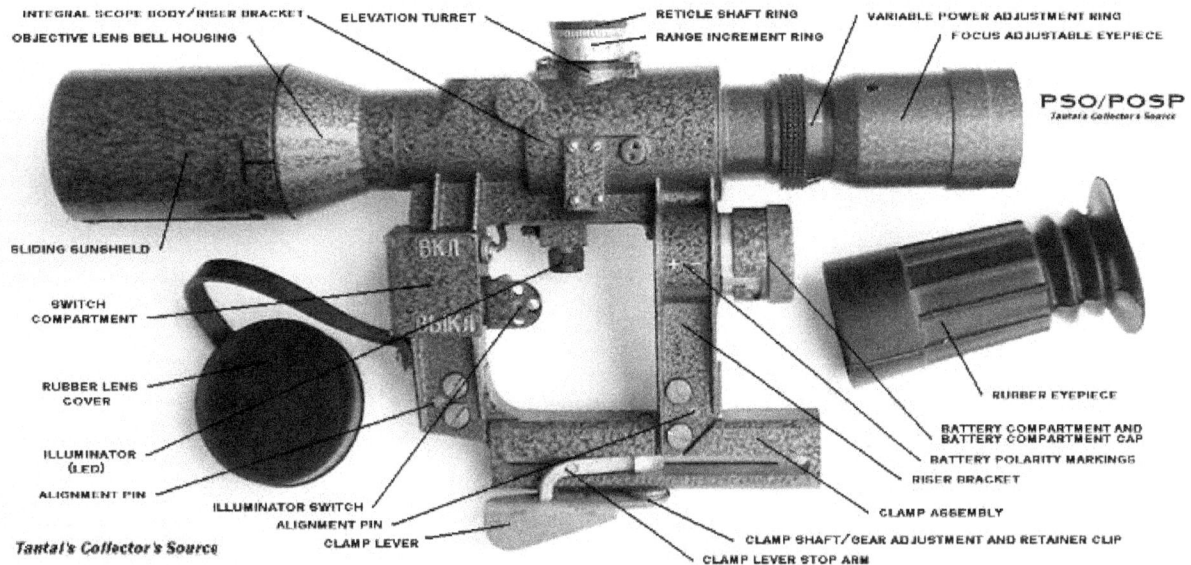

INTEGRAL SCOPE BODY/RISER BRACKET   ELEVATION TURRET   RETICLE SHAFT RING   VARIABLE POWER ADJUSTMENT RING
OBJECTIVE LENS BELL HOUSING   RANGE INCREMENT RING   FOCUS ADJUSTABLE EYEPIECE

PSO/POSP
Tantal's Collector's Source

SLIDING SUNSHIELD

SWITCH
COMPARTMENT

RUBBER LENS
COVER

ILLUMINATOR
(LED)

ALIGNMENT PIN

ILLUMINATOR SWITCH
ALIGNMENT PIN
CLAMP LEVER

Tantal's Collector's Source

RUBBER EYEPIECE

BATTERY COMPARTMENT AND
BATTERY COMPARTMENT CAP

BATTERY POLARITY MARKINGS

RISER BRACKET

CLAMP ASSEMBLY

CLAMP SHAFT/GEAR ADJUSTMENT AND RETAINER CLIP
CLAMP LEVER STOP ARM

Figure 1-12 POSP Scope Nomenclature

POSP Model Scopes

The PSO "V" style variant is specific to the AK series rifle and will provide the proper eye relief and attaching mechanism for most types of AK optic side plates. The designator "V" at the end of a scope description marks its mount for AK/Saiga/RPK weapons or AK- (V-suffix) type mounting clamps. Many units are equipped with an adjustable eyepiece diopter focus (D-suffix). Standard PSO-1 series models have a fixed or omni-focus design.

PSO-1

The SVD comes standard with a PSO-1 scope, a 4x24mm device which includes a battery-operated reticule and a passive infrared filter. At the time of its development, the PSO-1 scope was considered one of the most advanced sniper scope designs ever fielded. Its reticule consists of multiple aiming points (chevrons) that are used for distances beyond 1000 meters. There is also a rangefinder built into the reticule, which allows approximate distance calculations based on the height of an average human (which the Soviets felt was 1.7 meters tall).

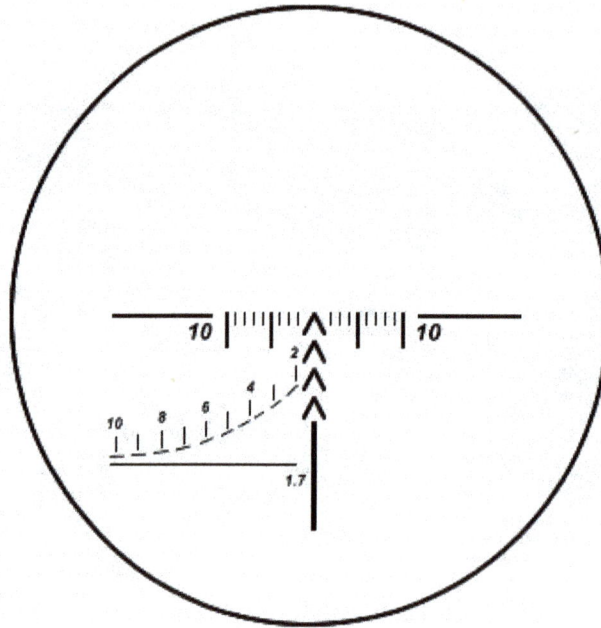

Figure 1-13a PSO-1 Reticle

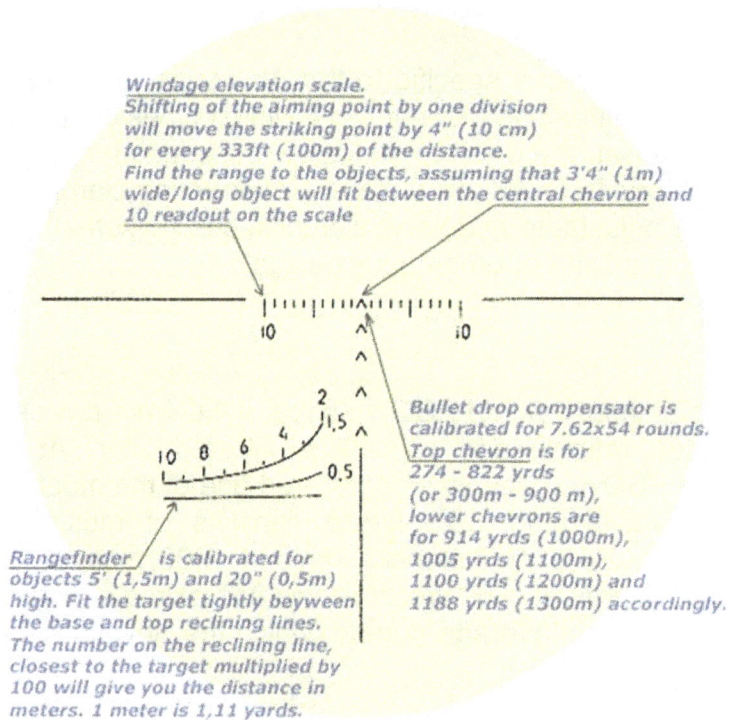

Windage elevation scale.
Shifting of the aiming point by one division
will move the striking point by 4" (10 cm)
for every 333ft (100m) of the distance.
Find the range to the objects, assuming that 3'4" (1m)
wide/long object will fit between the central chevron and
10 readout on the scale

Bullet drop compensator is
calibrated for 7.62x54 rounds.
Top chevron is for
274 - 822 yrds
(or 300m - 900 m),
lower chevrons are
for 914 yrds (1000m),
1005 yrds (1100m),
1100 yrds (1200m) and
1188 yrds (1300m) accordingly.

Rangefinder / is calibrated for
objects 5' (1,5m) and 20" (0,5m)
high. Fit the target tightly beyween
the base and top reclining lines.
The number on the reclining line,
closest to the target multiplied by
100 will give you the distance in
meters. 1 meter is 1,11 yards.

Figure 1-13b PSO-1 Reticle Explanation

Many other conventional and night-vision optics are available. In case of scope failure, the rifle has non-detachable iron sights, a feature that does not exist on many sniper rifles.

Reticle for 7.62x54R

Rangefinder- The rangefinder works by placing the target (1.7 meter/5'8" in height) between the horizontal and the top reclining line with numbers. On the reclining line, locate the number closest to the point where the target touches the line. Multiply that number by 100; this is the distance to the target in meters. 1 meter = 1.1 yards.

Windage scale- The windage scale can be used to make horizontal adjustments or as a range finder. Shifting the aiming point by one division left or right will move the point of impact by 10 cm (4") for every 100 meter/109 yards of the distance. The distance to the target can be determined by assuming that a 1 meter/3'4" wide/long object fits between the small divisions at 100 meter/109 yards.

Aiming chevrons- The chevrons are designed to adjust for bullet drop at 1,000, 1,100, and 1,200 meters, aiming with the 2nd, 3rd, and the 4th chevrons, respectively.

Figure 1-14c PSO Scope as issued

Issued scope kit:

- Sight with a cover of a lens
- Eye-shield
- Operation manual
- Case

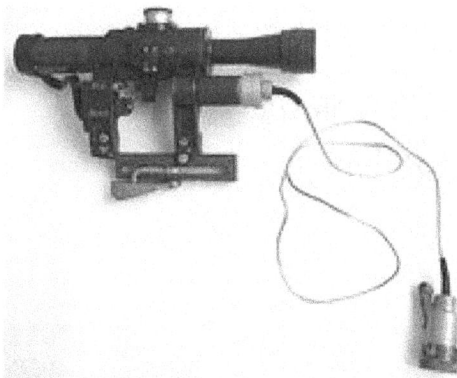

Figure 1-15d Remote power for cold weather (keeps batteries warm in jacket)

POSP 4x24M

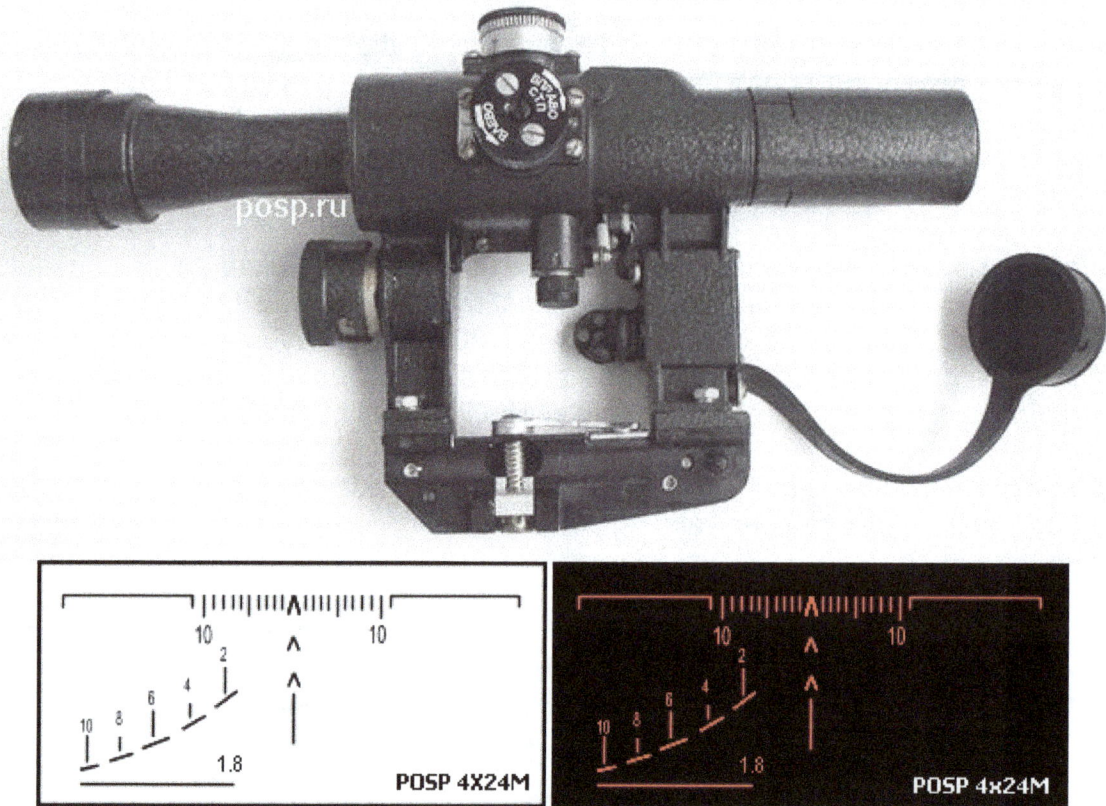

Figure 1-16 POSP 4x24 M, 7.62x54R Reticle and 1000-meter Rangefinder Scope

SPECIFICATIONS

Mountable on	**SVD/TIGR**
Type	4x24
Magnification	4x
Range finder	1000 meters
Operating temperature	-50°C/+50°C
Field of view (FOV), degrees	6
FOV@100m	7 meters
Objective diameter	24 mm
Powered by	1xCR1/3N or 2xD-357 (3V)
Weight	1.4 pounds/.62 kg
Length	13.3 inches/33.7cm

POSP 6x24M

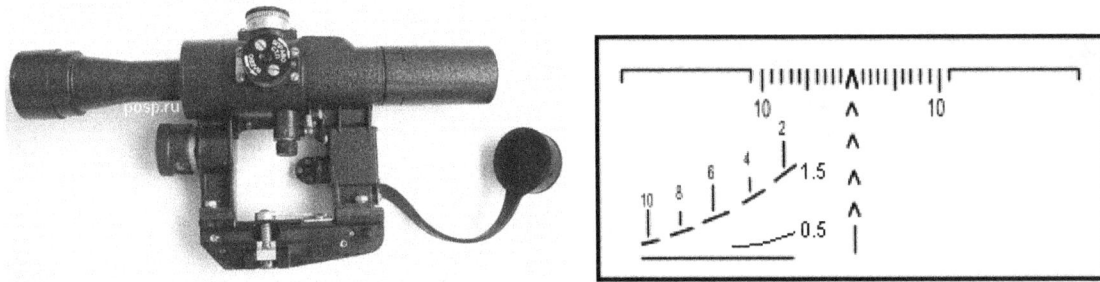

Figure 1-17 POSP 6x24, 1000-meter Rangefinder Scope and 7.62x54R Reticle

SPECIFICATIONS

Mountable on	**SVD/TIGR**
Type	6x42
Magnification	6x
Rangefinder	1000 meters
Operating temperature	-50°C/+50°C
Field of view (FOV), degrees	4
FOV@100m	6 meters
Objective diameter	24 mm
Powered by	1xCR1/3N or 2xD-357 (3V)
Weight	1.4 pounds/.62 kg
Length	13.3 inches/ 33.7cm

The PSO 6x24M is a higher-powered PSO-1, which provides a very happy medium for users needing additional magnification who prefer not to add additional weight and length or alter the rifle's original classic profile. It will also deliver superior accuracy when extended ranges are being used and employs the upgraded dual-gradient illuminated rangefinder of the 8x series scopes (see below). It has been a popular choice for those who need a moderate, inexpensive upgrade from the standard scope. Power for low-light and nighttime use is provided by common watch batteries and controlled by a weatherized toggle-switch assembly.

POSP 6x42

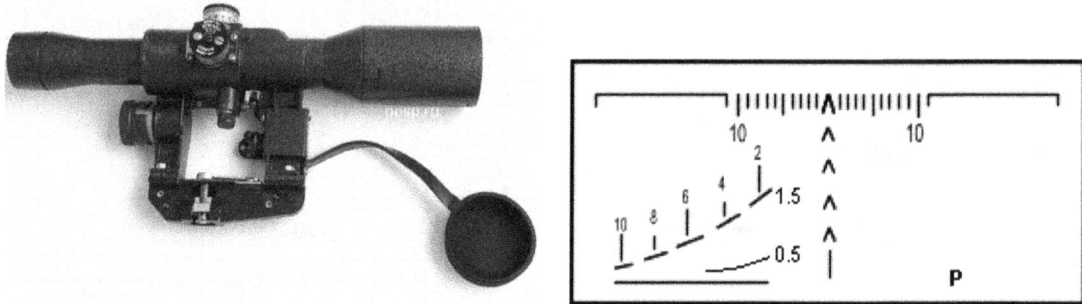

Figure 1-18 POSP 6x42, 1000-meter Rangefinder Scope and 7.62x54R Reticle

SPECIFICATIONS

Mountable on	**SVD/TIGR**
Type	6x42
Magnification	6x
Rangefinder	1000 meters
Operating temperature	-50°C/+50°C
Field of view (FOV), degrees	4
FOV@100m	5.2 meters
Objective diameter	42 mm
Powered by	1xCR1/3N or 2xD-357 (3V)
Weight	1.6 pounds/.73 kg
Length	16 inches/ 40.8 cm

An enlarged exit pupil and objective tube greatly improve the light-gathering ability of the PSO in night and low-light conditions, which means you will enjoy an improved, brighter field of view using this 42mm scope. Fully coated lenses and nitrogen-filled internals are always standard.

POPS 6x42D – 1000-meter range-finding and adjustable eyepiece scope

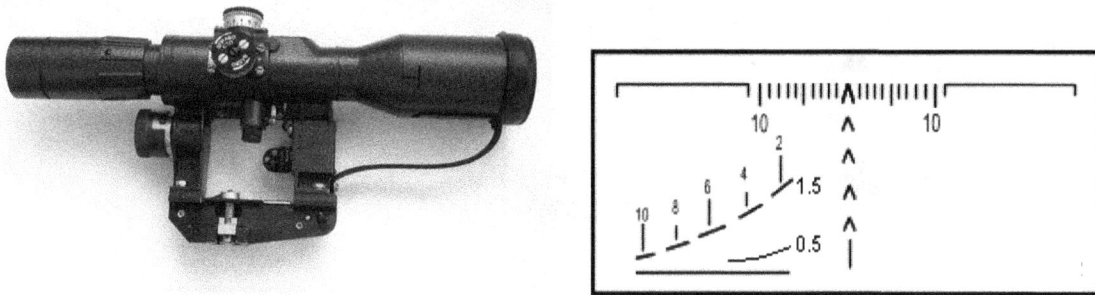

Figure 1-19 POSP 6x42D, 1000-meter Rangefinder Scope and 7.62x54R Reticle

SPECIFICATIONS

Mountable on	**SVD/TIGR**
Type	6x42
Magnification	6x
Rangefinder	1000 meters
Operating Temperature	-50°C/+50°C
Field of View (FOV), degrees	4
FOV@100m	7 meters
Objective Diameter	42 mm
Powered by	1xCR1/3N or 2xD-357 (3V)
Weight	1.9 pounds/.85 kg
Length	16 inches/40.6 cm

D denotes a special adjustable diopter focus eyepiece which enables the end user to adjust for his own personal vision.

POSP 8x42D

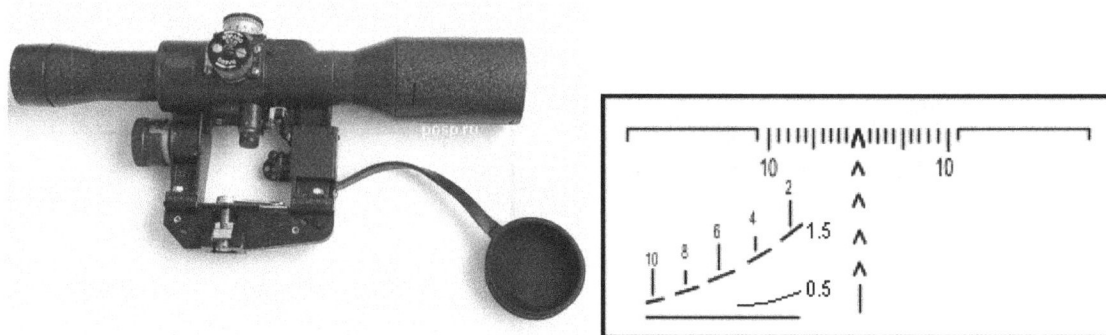

Figure 1-20 POSP 8x42D, 1000-meter Rangefinder Scope and 7.62x54R Reticle

SPECIFICATIONS

Mountable on	**SVD/TIGR**
Type	8x42
Magnification	8x
Rangefinder	1000 meters
Operating Temperature	-50°C/+50°C
Field of View (FOV), degrees	3
FOV@100m	5.2 meters
Objective Diameter	42 mm
Powered by	1xCR1/3N or 2xD-357 (3V)
Weight	1.7 pounds/.77 kg
Length	16 inches /40.6 cm

D denotes a special adjustable diopter focus eyepiece which enables the end user to adjust for his own personal vision.

PO 3-9x42M (military designation 1P21) – 1300-meter rangefinder and variable magnification

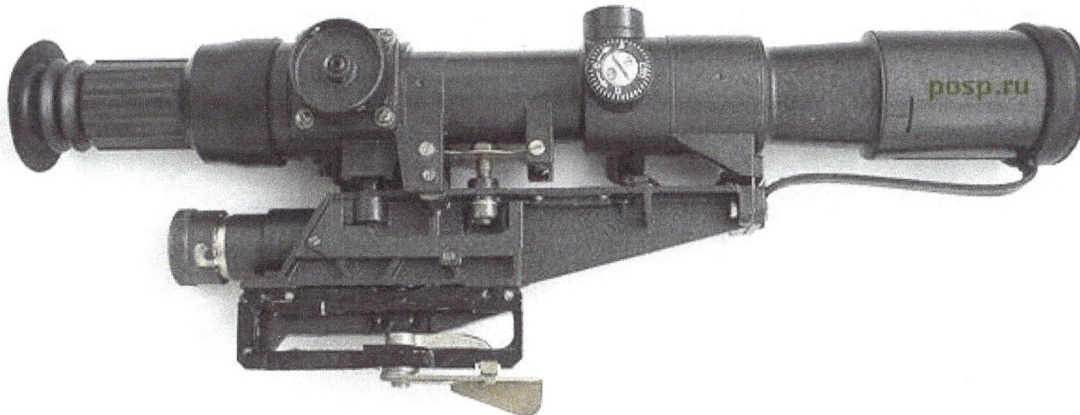

Figure 1-21a PO 3-9x42M, 1300-meter Rangefinder Scope

The current military issue 1P21 (PO 3-9x42) *Minuta* is modified for 2xLR44 (or 1xCR1/3N) 3V batteries. The scope has a magnesium alloy body, which is finished in a "military" dark-grey protective coating. The reticules are illuminated in red, making the contrasting reticule line free of glow, which allows it to be used in dusk conditions. The upper aiming chevron is designed to adjust for bullet drop from 300m to 900m. When the upper mark is zeroed for 900m (circular mark 9 brought to "12 o'clock" mark), the lower four chevrons are automatically zeroed for 1000, 1100, 1200, and 1300 meters. This scope is calibrated for the 7.62x54R SVD Dragunov rifle and is unique by its automatic bullet-drop compensation system. It comes in a waterproof pouch with rubber eyepiece and manual. Baseline zero of the sight is accomplished by the use of two recessed turret adjusters. Once zeroed, the sight uses a single knob-adjusting wheel for all three functions of zoom, range estimation, and angle of adjustment of the sight. Once the user zooms in to fit the target into a scale located on the rangefinder, the scope has already estimated the range. Range in hundreds of meters is indicated at the top of the sight reticle.

Although originally designed for the SVD Dragunov, the 1P21 *Minuta* uses the standard night-vision base-clamp system, which means it will fit all types of AK and SVD side plates to include the *Tigr*, NDM-86, *Vepr*, *Saiga*, Romanian SAR 1-3, *Romak* 1/2, PSL/Romak3, MPK, MTK, and others. This sight fits low to the receiver, lower than most PSO models.

SPECIFICATIONS

Mountable on	**SVD/TIGR**
Type	3-9x42
Magnification	3-9x
Rangefinder	1300 meters
Operating Temperature	-50°C/+50°C
Field of View (FOV), degrees	2.7-5
Powered by	1xCR1/3N or 2xD-357 (3V)
Weight	2.9 pounds /1.3 kg
Length	15.8 inches/40 cm

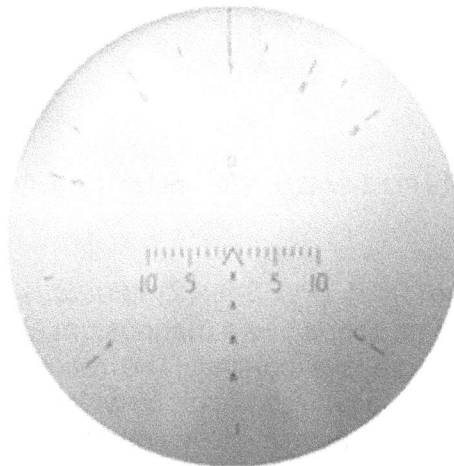

Figure 1-21b PO 3-9x42mm 7.62x54R Reticle

Once the scope's magnification dial mark 3 is set up on the 12 o'clock magnification readout mark and the scope is zeroed at 300m (330yds) distance, you can automatically determine the distance to the target and zero the upper chevron for distances of up to 900m (990yds), if the size measurements of the target are known and fit within the rectangular box. By rotating the magnification/range dial knob, you have to bring the target within the limits of the rectangular and horizontal line, which measure the height levels 0.75 - 1.5m and 0.5m width. The distance to the target is the number on the dial mark set on the 12 o'clock readout mark: 3 - 300m, 4 - 400m, 5 - 500m, and so on up to 9 - 900m. If the target size differs from the pre-set measurements of the rectangular box, you can calculate the distance and zero on the target by using the horizontal aiming scale. For example, if the width of the target is 2m and it fits within two horizontal marks, the distance to the target is 100m; if it fits in one mark, the distance is 200m. Each division of horizontal scale measures 1m width at 100m distance and can be used for windage correction by shifting the aiming point left or right by one division, which moves the point of impact by 10cm (4") at 100m (110yds) distance or 1m at 1000m distance.

Magnification/ Range dial marks; variable from 3 to 9 (300m - 900m)

Magnification readout mark

The rectangular box & horizontal line to measure the target and determine the distance

Horizontal windage scale

10   1000m ʌ   5   10
1100m ʌ
1200m ʌ
1300m ʌ

Bullet drop compensation chevrons; the upper chevron for 300m-900m zeroing; lower chevrons give correct compensation when magnification / range mark 9 is set on 12 o'clock readout mark

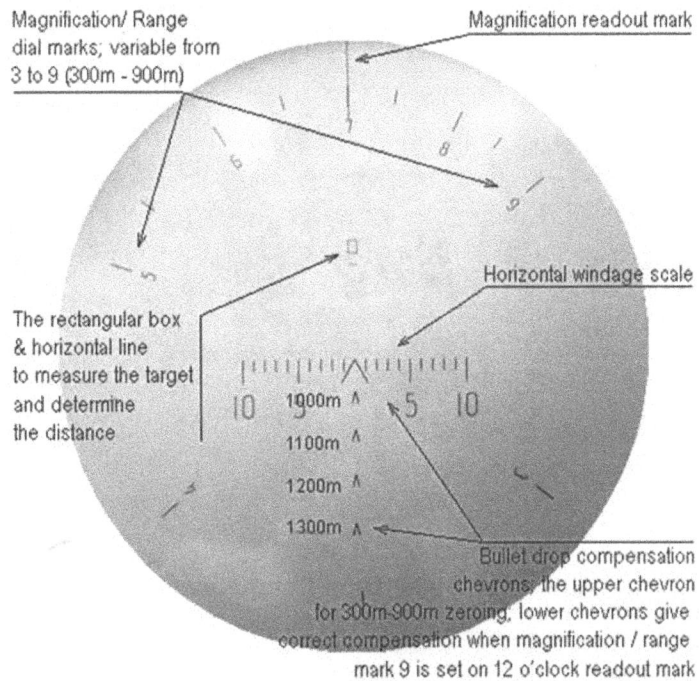

Figure 1-21c PO 3-9 x 42mm 7.62x54R Reticle Explanation

PO 4-12x42

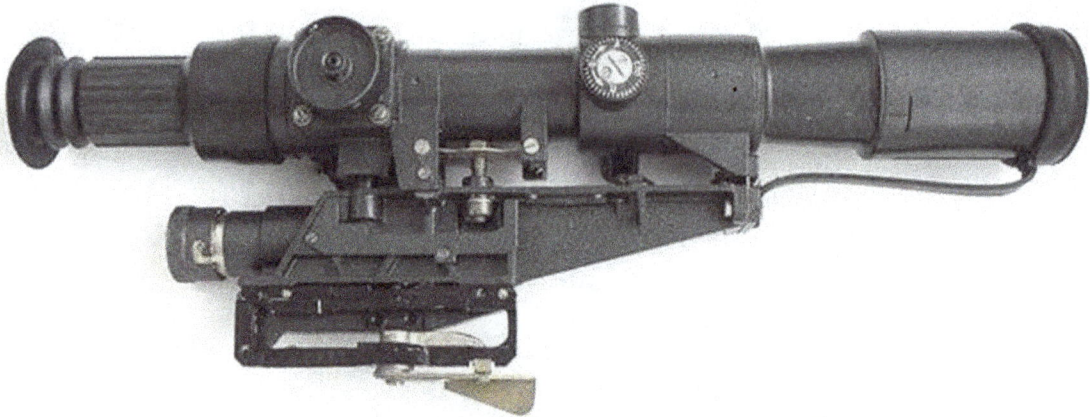

Figure 1-22 PO 4-12x42 - Automatic Bullet-Drop Compensation and Variable Magnification Scope

SPECIFICATIONS

Mountable on	**SVD/TIGR**
Type	4-12x42
Magnification	4-12x
Rangefinder	1300 meters
Operating Temperature	-50°C/+50°C
Field of View (FOV), degrees	2-5
FOV@100m	3.5-7 meters
Objective Diameter	42 mm
Powered by	1xCR1/3N or 2xD-357 (3V)
Weight	2.9 pounds/1.3 kg
Length	15.8 inches /40 cm

Night Vision Devices (NVD) for SVD Rifles

Figure 1-23 1PN-51 NVD

Figure 1-24 Old version- 1PN-58 NVD

Mount Identification

Figure 1-25a Type 1- Dragunov

Figure 1-25b Type 2- AKM

Type-1 or Dragunov-style mounting clamp found on the POSP-type rifle scope has a forward-placed stop pin. The clamp has to slide all the way forward on the rail, with the pin being guided by the groove in the rail until it catches the closed end of the groove in the left most position. REMEMBER that the scopes with the Type-1 mounting clamp will properly fit the plate on your rifle ONLY if the front end of the groove is CLOSED. A closed middle grove won't allow the scope to come off at the other end of the rail, and the scope will always retain its "zero."

Type-2 (AK type) mounting clamp has the rear-placed stop pin and is designed to fit mounting plates found on AK, Saiga, and Vepr rifles. The clamp has to slide forward on the rail until it is stopped as the pin comes against the back (right) end of the mounting plate. REMEMBER that the scopes with the AK/Saiga-type mounting clamp will properly fit the plate on your rifle ONLY if the plate has a CLOSED right end of the rail. This mount places the scope a little higher on the weapon and not as far forward as the Type-1 mounts.

Mounting Clamp Adjustments

Step 1: Invert the sight and notice the retaining clip that is holding the lever onto the sight. Place a small screwdriver blade on the edge of the retaining clip, and by using the thumb lever as a pivot, rotate the retainer out of its detent. In the field, you can hold the sight steady by placing it between your knees.

Ammunition

The 7.62x54mm Russian/Rimmed ammunition used by the SVD is produced by Russia, former Soviet republics, China, and many different European countries. The 7.62x54mm R cartridges will be encountered in both brass and steel cases; however, steel cases are more prolific. The <u>7.62mm</u> is the diameter of the bullet, <u>54mm</u> is the length of the case, and <u>R</u> represents Russian or Rimmed.

The SVD is chambered for the 7.62x54R rimmed cartridge, with a muzzle velocity of about 830 meters per second (mps)/2,723 feet per second (fps). The rifle can fire the older Mosin Nagant M1891/30 cartridge, but a more accurate 7N1 round was designed specifically for use in the SVD. The 7N1 was the original load developed by Russian armorers in conjunction with the development of the SVD back in the late 1950s. It has a steel-jacketed projectile with an air pocket, steel core, and a lead core in the base for maximum terminal effect. The 7N1 was replaced in 1999 by the improved 7N14 round. It consists of a 151-grain projectile which travels at the same 830 mps/2723 fps, but it has a lead-core projectile and is more accurate. However, the Soviet Union never offered this ammunition for export, and it is very rare outside of Russia. This ammunition can be identified by its packaging which has in Russian *Снайперские* (Sniper) stamped on its crates, cans, and paper wrap to prevent it from being wasted in other weapon applications.

Although the rifle is lethal at ranges above 1000 m, it is not really intended or designed for ultimate accuracy and can only reasonably engage targets at up to 600 m with standard ammunition, achieving two minutes of arc at that distance. This range and accuracy can be improved with the specialty ammunition. Inaccuracy in this weapon is primarily due to the effects of the semiautomatic action of the SVD on the barrel harmonics; the accuracy of the rifle suffers at greater ranges. However, the weapon handles easily for its size and is designed to be very durable; the gas system and bore are chrome lined to resist corrosion, and it is easy to clean. The rifle also has a bayonet lug for close-quarters combat, although the mounting of a bayonet will cause a slight change in the center of gravity, affecting the handling qualities of the rifle, and possibly accuracy.

The following is a brief list of the different types of ammunition and their uses:

- *Снайперские* (Sniper) 7N1 FMJ ball: 1 MOA – a 151-grain projectile with a muzzle velocity of 830 m/s/2723 fps. Externally, the 7N1 looks identical to standard steel-cased LPS ball ammunition. There is no color coding on the bullet tip or primer annulus, and no specialized head stamp.

- *Снайперские* (Sniper) 7N14 FMJ ball: 0.75 MOA – 151-grain projectile with a muzzle velocity of 830 m/s/2723 fps, a new sniper round. The new dedicated sniper load was placed into production in 1999. This new load replaces the 7N1, which had been operational with Russian forces since 1966. All Russian 7.62x54R Sniper and Match ammunition is produced by

Factory 188, also known as the Novosibirsk Low-Voltage Equipment Plant. The 7N14 was developed to provide the Russian sniper with an armor-piercing bullet with the accuracy of a match cartridge to overcome the proliferation of modern body armor. The new load features a steel-jacketed .311 diameter 152-grain FMJBT projectile with an AP core. Cases are copper-washed steel with corrosive Berdan priming. The trajectory coincides with the older 7N1. Penetration, though, is substantially improved over the older load. As an example, when fired at a 10mm-thick grade-3 steel plate placed at 250m, the 7N14 achieved 100% penetration while the 7N1 was defeated. There is no color coding on the bullet tip or primer annulus, and no specialized head stamp.

- LPS FMJ ball: 2 MOA – Steel-core ball - for use against light material targets, personnel, or training. The steel-core ball weighs 148 grains and has a muzzle velocity of 825 m/s (2700 fps). No tip markings.

Figure 1-26 Steel-core ammunition

- Type D Steel-core ball – for use against light material targets, personnel, or training. The steel core ball weighs 182 grains and has a muzzle velocity of 825 m/s (2700 fps). Tip markings on the bullet are yellow.

- T-46 tracer: 2 MOA – Tracer - for observation of fire, incendiary effects, signaling, and use during training. The range of a tracer was required to be 1500 meters, but was actually closer to 1200 meters. The tracer compound was a mix of barium salts, magnesium, and aluminum. Green-tipped marking denotes the green trace when fired.

Figure 1-27 Tracer ammunition

- 7N13 AP: 1.2 MOA – Armor piercing - for use against lightly armored targets where armor-piercing effects are desired. Black-tipped marking.

Figure 1-28 Armor-piercing ammunition

- Armor piercing-incendiary – for desired armor-piercing effects combined with fire producing/incendiary effects. Tip markings are black and red or purple.

- Blank – for use during training when simulating live fire. If blanks are to be fired from the PKM machine gun, a blank adapter must first be fitted to the muzzle. Without the blank adapter, insufficient gas pressure is generated to cycle the weapon properly. Crimped purple nose.

Figure 1-29 Blank ammunition

Ammunition Packaging

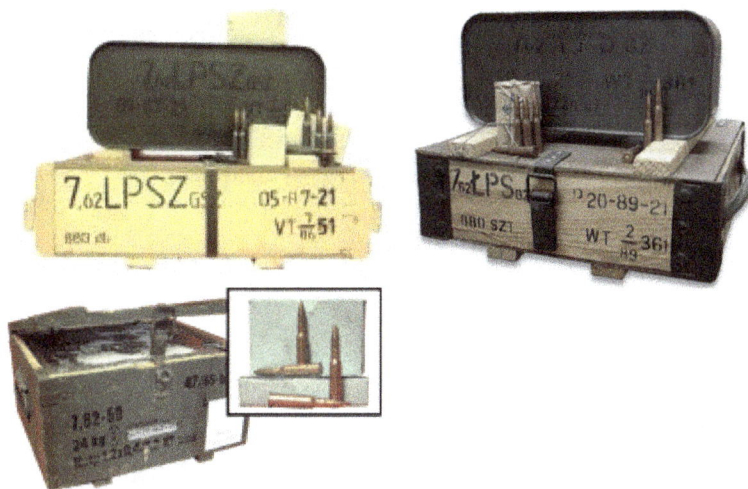

LPS Hungarian packaging   LPS Polish packaging   LPS Czech packaging

Figure 1-30 Various low-grade LPS ammunition packaging

Sniper Grade Packaging – To identify this load, it must be in its original packaging as factories also produce ball ammunition at the same location. It comes packed 20 rounds to a paper packet, 22 packets to a metal tin, two tins per wooden case for a total of 880 rounds. The wooden shipping crates, hermetically sealed metal "spam" cans, and individual paper packets are all distinctly marked *Снайперские* "SNIPER" in Cyrillic.

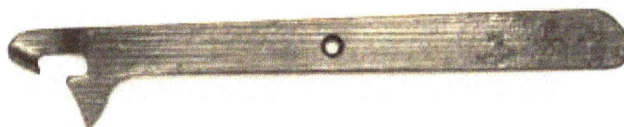

Figure 1-31 Ammunition can opener

Metal can opener used to open the sardine-style metal cans. One opener will be in each wooden crate that contains the two metal ammo cans. Without it, opening the cans is quite an adventure; we have used Leatherman tools, chisels, and bayonets. If using a bayonet or other non-designed can opener, be careful not to beat a bayonet tip into one of the primers.

Ammunition Identification

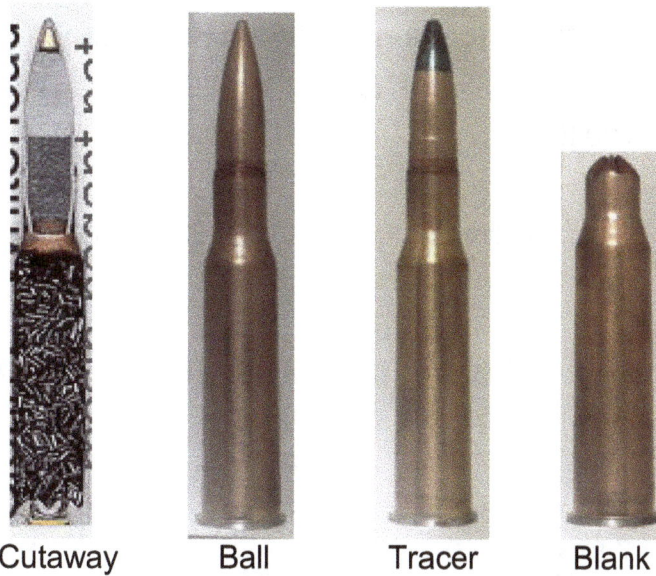

| Cutaway | Ball | Tracer | Blank |

Figure 1-32 Various ammunition examples

Caliber, mm	Case	Bullet type	Bullet, wt. Gram/grain	Primer Type	Description
7.62x54R	Bimetal	Bimetal	9.6/148	Berdan	Steel Core
7.62x54R	Bimetal	Tracer T-46	9.65/149	Berdan	Tracer Bullet
7.62x54R	Bimetal	None	None	Berdan	Blank

7.62x54 R Ballistic Chart

7.62x54 R 148-grain Ball Ammunition

BC: 0.398   CALIBER: 0.308 inch/7.62mm   WEIGHT: 148 grain /9.6 grams

Muzzle Velocity: 2700 ft/s

WS: 10 mph

Temperature: 59 °F   Barometric Pressure: 29.92 in Hg

Range	Bullet Drop		Wind		Lead	
(meters)	(inches)	(MOA)	(inches)	(MOA)	(inches)	(MOA)
100	6.4	5.6	1.0	0.9	22.4	19.5
200	7.4	3.2	4.4	1.9	47.0	20.5
300	-0.0	-0.0	10.4	3.0	74.4	21.6
400	-17.8	-3.9	19.5	4.2	104.8	22.9
500	-48.5	-8.5	32.1	5.6	138.7	24.2
600	-95.3	-13.9	48.8	7.1	176.8	25.7
700	-162.5	-20.3	70.1	8.7	219.4	27.4
800	-254.8	-27.8	96.1	10.5	266.7	29.1
900	-377.9	-36.7	126.6	12.3	318.5	30.9
1000	-537.2	-46.9	161.1	14.1	374.3	32.7
1100	-737.7	-58.6	198.9	15.8	433.5	34.4
1200	-984.2	-71.6	239.8	17.5	495.7	36.1
1300	-1281.4	-86.1	283.7	19.1	560.9	37.7
1400	-1633.7	-101.9	330.3	20.6	628.8	39.2
1500	-2046.0	-119.1	379.7	22.1	699.6	40.7

7.62x54 R Ballistic Chart

NOTE: Minute of Angle (MOA): The term Minute of Angle, referred to as MOA, is actually a unit of measure dealing with circles found in surveying, navigation, and mathematics. One Minute of Angle is 1/60th of one degree of a circle. A circle has 360 degrees, and 21,600 Minutes of Angle are in a circle.

If you were to look at a circle which has a radius of 100 yards and project lines out from the center in Minute of Angle increments, you would find that at 100 yards away from the center of the circle, the distance between the Minute of Angle lines would be 1.0472 inches.

Over time, one Minute of Angle at 100 yards has been rounded off to one inch and has become a standard unit of measurement for bullet trajectory calculations, comparisons, accuracy levels, and the sighting-in of firearms.

The chart below illustrates the Minute of Angle concept and plots what one, two, and three Minutes of Angle would be at various distances.

One, Two and Three Minute of Angle (MOA) Chart

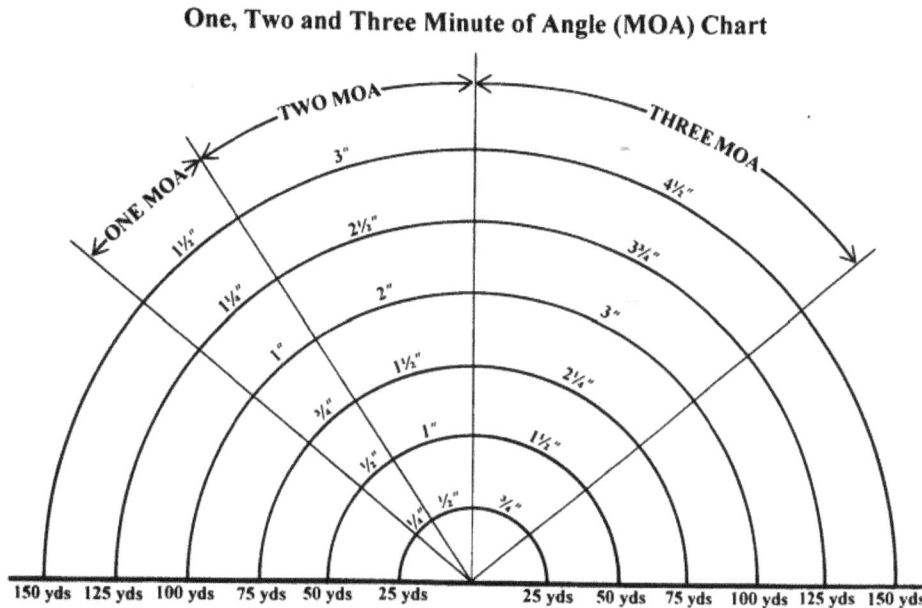

Figure 1-33 MOA Chart

The chart below shows another viewpoint of how Minute of Angle measurements apply to firearms and accuracy. Frequently, a weapon's accuracy is described as being able to fire groups that are less than one Minute of Angle at 100 yards, meaning that if the shooter fired five rounds at a target 100 yards away and used correct sight alignment, the group would measure less than one inch.

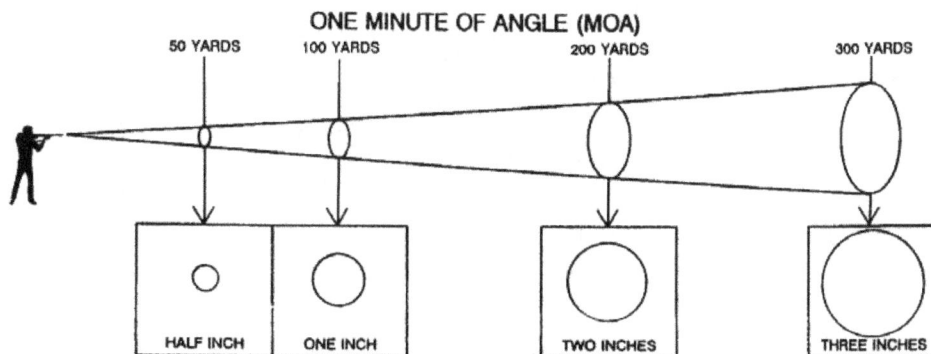

Figure 1-34 MOA Chart

Section 2

Nomenclature and Maintenance

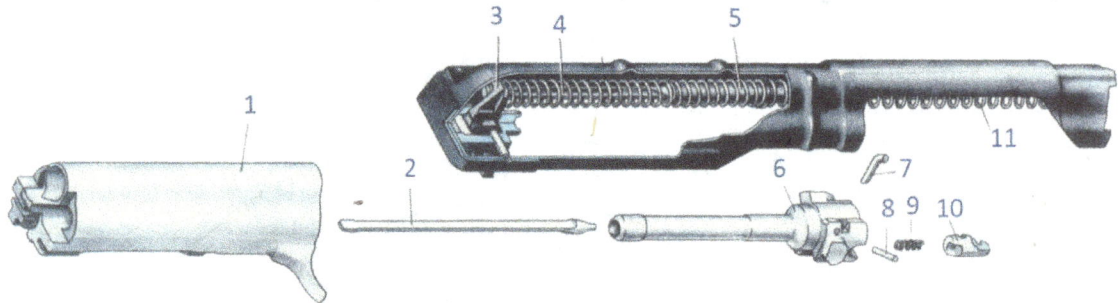

Figure 2-1a Exploded Diagram of the SVD Bolt Carrier Assembly and Receiver Cover

1- Bolt carrier
2- Firing Pin
3- Boss Latch
4- Recoil Spring

5- Guide Rod
6- Bolt
7- Extractor Pin
8- Firing Pin Retaining Pin

9- Extractor Spring
10- Extractor
11- Receiver Cover

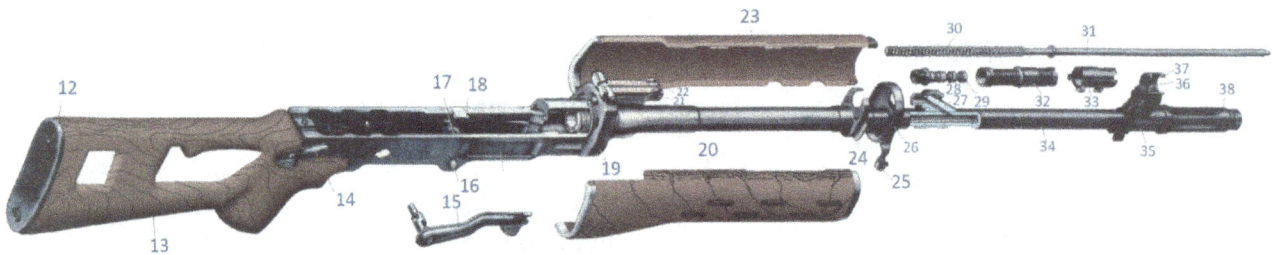

Figure 2-1b Exploded Diagram of the SVD

12- Butt Plate
13- Buttstock
14- Dustcover Locking Latch
15- Safety Lever
16- Cross Bridge Dowel
17- Receiver
18- Ejector
19- Rear Retaining Band
20- Handguard, Right

21- Rear Sight Base
22- Rear Sight
23- Handguard, Left
24- Fixed Retaining Band
25- Retaining Band Lock
26- Moveable Retaining Band
27- Gas Block
28- Gas Tube Lock
29- Gas Piston

30- Driving Rod Spring
31- Driving Rod
32- Gas Tube
33- Gas Regulator
34- Barrel
35- Front Sight Post
36- Front Sight
37- Front Sight Guard
38- Flash Suppressor

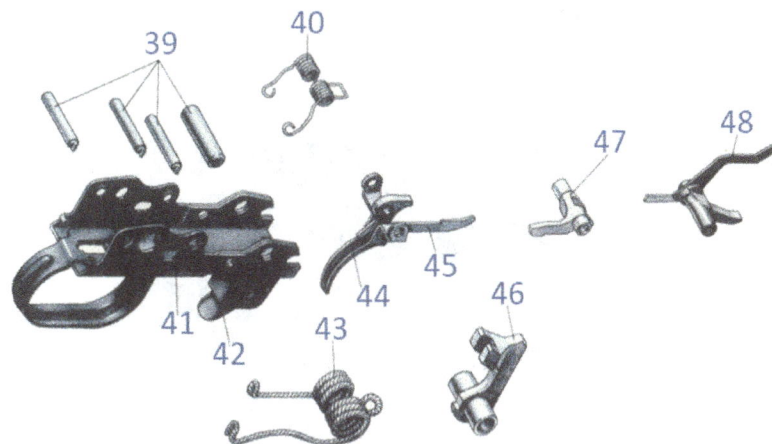

Figure 2-1c Exploded Diagram of the SVD Trigger Group

39- Assembly Pins
40- Trigger Spring
41- Trigger Housing
42- Magazine Release

43- Hammer Spring
44- Trigger
45- Trigger Bar

46- Hammer
47- Sear
48- Auto Sear

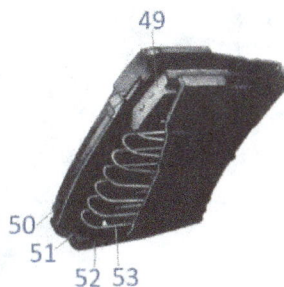

Figure 2-1d Exploded Diagram of the SVD Magazine

49- Magazine Follower
50- Magazine Body

51- Retainer Plate
52- Magazine Floorplate

53- Magazine Spring

Clearing the SVD Rifle

Figure 2-2 SVD Safety

A. Ensure the rifle is on "**SAFE**" with the safety lever up and the rifle is pointed in a safe direction, Figure 2-2.

Figure 2-3

B. Remove the magazine by pressing the magazine catch to the front and rotate the magazine forward from the magazine well in the rifle (Figure 2-3). Place the magazine in a pocket or magazine pouch or set it down.

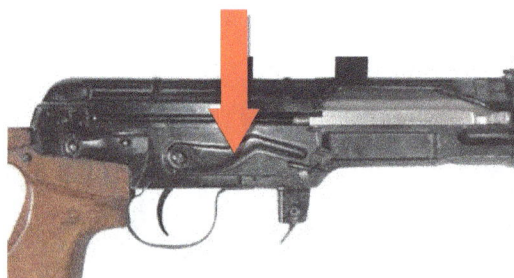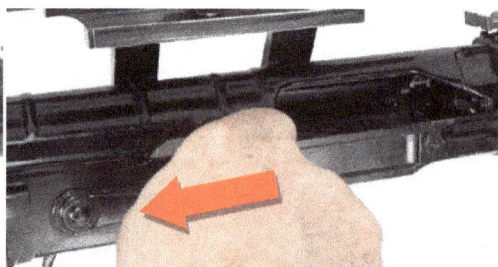

Figure 2-4a   **Figure 2-4b**

C. 1- Place the rifle's safety lever on "**FIRE**" and then grip the charging handle on the bolt carrier (Figure 2-4a) and 2- pull the bolt carrier rearward (Figure 2-4b), allowing the round to extract and eject from the rifle. 3- observe the round extracting and ejecting from the ejection port; do not attempt to retain the round.

D. Visually check the chamber for a stuck round. Once you have ensured the rifle has no magazine in it and the chamber is free of a round, you now can close the action by riding the bolt carrier forward and not by its own spring tension so as not to shut on an empty chamber forcefully.

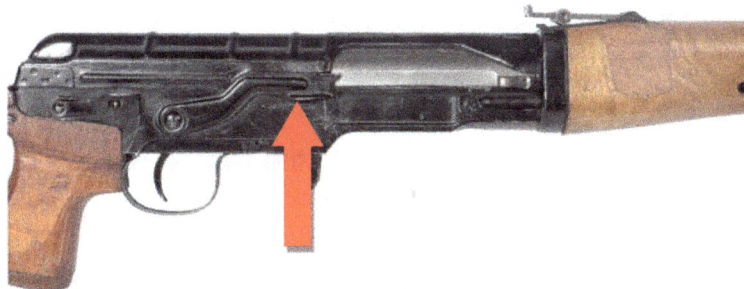

Figure 2-6

E. Place the rifle on "**SAFE**" (up position), Figure 2-6.

Disassembling the SVD Rifle

NOTE- Place the rifle's parts on a flat, clean surface with the muzzle oriented in a safe direction.

When the operator begins to disassemble the rifle, it should be done in the following order:

A. Clear the rifle and leave the magazine out and safety OFF.

B. To remove the scope from the receiver rail,

    1. Rotate the tension lever on the scope mount to the rear of the rifle.

    2. Once the tension lever is released, slide the mount to the rear and off the receiver rail.

    3. Place the scope aside where it cannot be dropped or damaged.
C. Remove the slide and driving spring.

1. Slightly pull out on the dustcover locking latch to get the latch off the locking tit, and rotate it down and towards the rear of the rifle (Figures 2-8a and 2-8b).

Figure 2-8a   **Figure 2-8b**

2. Lift the dustcover up and to the rear to remove it and the recoil spring assembly (Figure 2-9).

Figure 2-9

3. Once the dust cover assembly is clear of the rifle, slide the bolt carrier assembly to the rear and out of the receiver, Figure 2-10.

Figure 2-10

4. Remove the bolt from the bolt carrier by turning the bolt to the right and out of the carrier lug recess, Figure 2-11.

Figure 2-11

5. To remove the handguards, press into the barrel band locking lever to allow it to pivot forward and down 180 degrees, Figures 2-12a and 2-12b.

Figure 2-12a

Figure 2-12b

6. Pull the barrel band forward towards the muzzle, Figure 2-13.

Figure 2-13

7. Lift up on the left and right handguard and remove, Figures 2-14a and 2-14b. Always fully inspect the barrel for damage or sabotage.

Figure 2-14a

Figure 2-14b

8. To dissemble the gas piston system, grasp the (ROD) behind the gas piston and retract it against the spring tension and lift up lightly

(Figure 2-15a), and once it is above the piston, remove it towards the muzzle and out from the rifle, Figure 2-15b.

 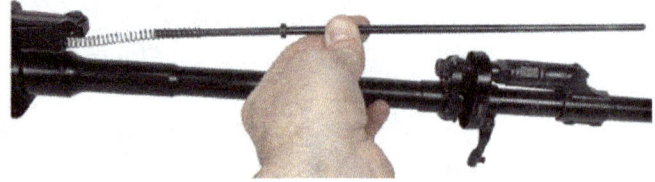

Figure 2-15a   **Figure 2-15b**

9. Grasp the knurled portion of the gas piston and remove it from the piston tube, Figure 2-16.

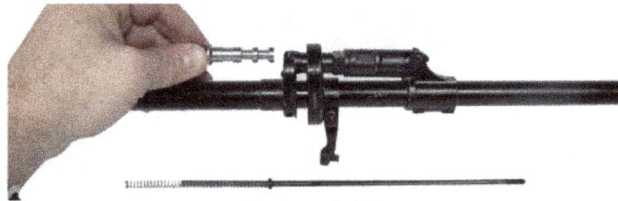

Figure 2-16

NOTE: The trigger assembly may be removed from the receiver but should be left to armorers who have been trained in the maintenance of the SVD at the depot level.

Cleaning and Lubrication

The SVD is to be cleaned and lubricated as any of the AK-type firearms. While cleaning, continually inspect all parts for damage or excessive wear and replace as required. The below listed issued cleaning kit is sufficient to properly maintain the rifle in the field. While in the basecamp you can use a standard 7.62 type cleaning system either J. Dewey or a Boresnake type system. Remember when lubricating the rifle, once it is clean use minimal lubricants and only in places where there is metal-on-metal contact during operation of the rifle. An overall light coat of oil will prevent rust but can also attract dust, so use as needed for the operating environment.

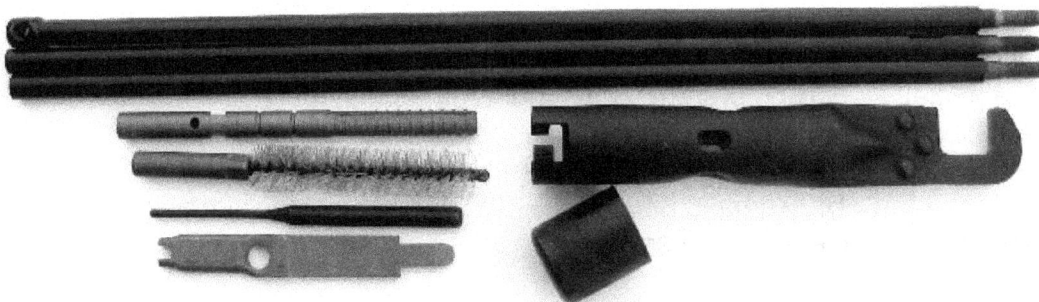

Figure 2-17 Cleaning Kit Components

1 - Cleaning rods
2 - Jag
3 - Brush
4 - Punch Tool

5- Screwdriver/Front Sight Tool
6- Bore Guide/Tube Cap
7- Combination Tool/Kit Carrier Tube

1- Cleaning rods- used for cleaning and lubricating the bore and chamber of the barrel while using a screw-on jag or brush. One end of a rod has a slot cut for using a patch. One end has a head which allows you to run it through the tool/tube for use as a "T" handle. Three sections are in each kit.
2- Jag- used to wrap a patch on for powder solvents or clean patches for cleaning the bore.
3- Brush- used to apply powder solvents at the beginning of the cleaning of the bore. Clean this brush once you are done with it so you do not introduce more fouling when using it later.
4- Punch Tool- used to push pins in the disassembly of the bolt, bolt carrier, and trigger housing unit.
5- Screwdriver/Front Sight Adjustment Tool- used to disassemble the rifle, clean the gas chamber and gas tube, and adjust the elevation on the front iron sight. This tool is fitted with the storage tube to be used as a handle to raise or lower the front sight. This tool can be used as a scraper for removing carbon fouling on parts. The hole in the middle of this tool is used in conjunction with the punch.
6- Bore Guide/Tube Cap- used to guide the cleaning rod into the bore from the muzzle end. Carefully insert the rod into the muzzle so as not to damage

the barrel crown. Slotted so it locks on to the storage tube to contain the small accessories.

7- Combination Tool/Kit Carrier Tube- used as a multi-function tool and the primary storage device for the other pieces in the kit, minus the rod sections.
   a. used as the cleaning rod handle by running the cleaning rods through it once they are assembled (two circulator holes)
   b. used as a handle for the screwdriver tool/sight tool, (two oval holes)
   c. used for cleaning the gas chamber and gas tube
   d. used as a spanner wrench for removing of the gas tube for cleaning
   e. has notches on it for assembling the rod sections.

Original Russian Izhmash-Manufactured military cleaning kits -- These new cleaning kits include a gray phosphate-finished bore brush, spiral jag, pin punch tool, special sight/gas system adjusting tool, black tubular case with hooked extension tool, and matching rotary-locking cap. These rare cleaning kits fit inside the top pocket of the original military magazine pouches. These can also be used with Romanian PSL/Romak3 and other 762x54R rifles. Use in conjunction with our original Russian cleaning rod sets.

Reassembling the SVD Rifle

Reverse the disassembly procedures to assemble the rifle and lubricate as required.

Performing a Function Check on the SVD

A. Clear the weapon as previously described to ensure it is unloaded.

B. Rotate the safety upward to the "**SAFE**" position.

B. Press the trigger (the hammer not fall).

C. Rotate the safety downward into the "**FIRE**" position.

D. Press the trigger and hold it to the rear (the hammer should fall).

E. Cycle the action to cock the hammer and release the trigger (the hammer should not fall).

F. Press the trigger to the rear (the hammer should fall).

G. Place the safety upward into the "**SAFE**" position.

H. If the hammer falls while on "**SAFE**" or fails to drop on "**FIRE**" during this function test, turn it in for repair.

Section 3

Operation and Function

Loading the SVD Magazine

A. Ensure you have the appropriate SVD ammunition; this ammunition is easily confused with other large-caliber ammunition. Inspect it for uniformity, cleanliness, and serviceability. Check all cartridges for undented primers and only use issued ammunition.

B. Use your non-dominant hand to hold the magazine with the rounded front of the magazine towards your fingertips. Your non-dominant thumb is used as a guide so as not to let the cartridge roll off the follower or other cartridges. With your dominant hand, one at a time, begin with the base of the cartridge at the front of the magazine follower and press the cartridge down and back to insert.

C. The magazine can hold 10 cartridges but due to overloading of the spring, do not carry the rifle in this configuration. Load 10 and then load the chamber so you have nine in the magazine and one in the chamber. Placing a cartridge in the chamber and releasing the bolt can cause damage to the extractor, so load the chamber from the magazine only.

Loading the SVD Rifle

A. Begin by clearing the rifle as previously described and perform a function test as necessary.

B. With the rifle pointed in a safe direction, place the rifle on "**SAFE**" (raise the safety lever) (Figure 3-2).

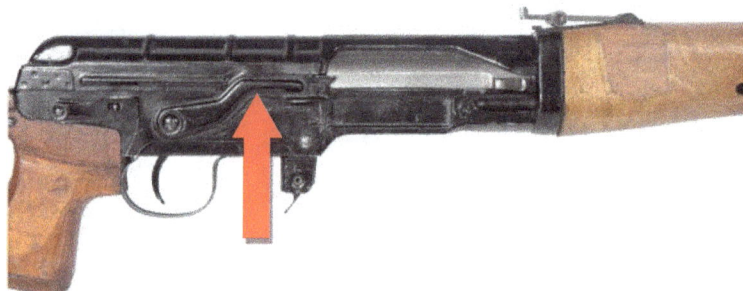

Figure 3-2

C. Lock the front of the loaded magazine into the front of the magazine well (identical to the AK series of rifles) and rotate the magazine up and to the rear until it locks into place (Figure 3-3a). Tug on the magazine to ensure lock up (Figure 3-3b).

Figure 3-3a

Figure 3-3b

D. Place the safety lever on "**FIRE**".

E. Pull the charging handle by gripping the handle and pulling the bolt carrier fully to the rear and then release so it strips a round from the magazine and goes into battery under its own spring tension (Figures 3-4a and 3-4b).

Figure 3-4a

Figure 3-4b

F. To ensure that a round has been chambered, perform a press check to observe the chambered casing through the ejection port. Ensure the bolt carrier is fully forward after conducting a press check as this will cause a failure-to-fire malfunction if not properly completed.

G. Return the rifle's safety lever to the "**SAFE**" position - upward (Figure 3-6).

Figure 3-6

Firing the SVD Rifle

A. Orient downrange or towards the threat.

B. Obtain proper sight alignment/scope eye relief, proper sight picture on the intended target.

C. Push down on the safety lever to place it on "**FIRE**".

Figure 3-7

D. As you maintain an acceptable hold with your sights on the target, press the trigger straight back so as not to interrupt the sight picture. Continue this straight-to-the-rear trigger pressure until the rifle fires.

E. Between a series of multiple shots, maintain finger-to-trigger contact and only allow forward trigger travel, which allows the mechanism to reset for the next shot.

F. When you have completed firing the rifle, place the safety lever into the "**SAFE**" (up) position.

Section 4

Performance Problems

Malfunction and Immediate Action Procedures

Malfunctions are usually preventable through good practices, but they may still occur out of the blue from time to time. Of course, you hope it is on the practice range, but you should treat each one as if you are in a life-or-death situation. Practicing proper and effective corrective actions will allow you to be more confident in your rifle handling. In stressful situations, you can become much more stressed due to an unforeseen malfunction that is easy to correct. I have observed many shooters that perceive themselves to be experienced, but when they encounter a stovepipe, they nearly disassemble the rifle rather than sweep it out and continue.

Malfunction drills must fix the problem 100% of the time (excluding a weapon stoppage—broken weapon) the first time performed. You must look at the rifle and identify the problem (obviously the rifle is not functioning as you need it to, so you must transition to another weapon or rectify the situation). It is a non-functioning weapon at this point—fix it.

You should always practice taking a covered position to correct malfunctions with considerations on how you operate.

The following pages in this chapter describe and detail corrective actions for the various malfunctions that may be encountered.

NOTE: The <u>failure-to-go-into-battery malfunction</u>, when your bolt does not fully return forward when cycling a round, is always rectified in the same manner, no matter which hand is being used. This malfunction is usually induced when loading and not allowing the full recoil spring tension to shut the slide.

To fix a failure-to-go-into-battery malfunction, you must ensure your finger is off the trigger and outside the triggerguard and then slap the back of the charging handle with the heel of the firing hand. If you are shooting while wounded, then you will use hard-structure items or equipment to force the bolt forward into battery.

<u>FAILURE TO FIRE</u>: This malfunction occurs when the operator has loaded a dud cartridge or failed to load the chamber. The universal fix all for this is the "<u>Rack, Bang</u>" technique.

SYMPTOM - You attempt to shoot and hear and feel the hammer strike, but the weapon does not fire.

1. RACK the charging handle fully to the rear with your firing hand and release it to shut by its own recoil spring tension; maintain muzzle to threat orientation.

2. BANG or reorient your sights onto the target and prepare to fire the shot as you intended before the malfunction if your situation dictates that action.

FAILURE TO EJECT: This malfunction (commonly called a "stovepipe") is usually created by the bolt carrier being retarded (by not holding the rifle tight enough to allow it to cycle properly) in its rearward movement to rechamber the next round or by a broken ejector. This malfunction is easily corrected by sweeping the expended case from the port.

SYMPTOM - You are in the act of shooting a multiple-round engagement, and you felt that the slide did not fully close, and/or you have a soft, mushy trigger.

With the firing hand reach up and pull the empty casing from the rifle without fully cycling the action.

Once the casing is no longer pinched by the bolt, the bolt will continue to seat the next round, and you are now ready to continue the engagement. Many inexperienced shooters do too much to correct this simple malfunction. **Ensure you do not work the bolt carrier fully to the rear when sweeping the empty casing -- this action could induce a double feed as the chamber is already loaded**. Continue the engagement as your situation dictates.

FAILURE TO EXTRACT: This malfunction (commonly called a "double feed") is created when the spent casing is not extracted from the chamber, and the next round to be loaded is rammed from the magazine into the rear of the stuck casing, This malfunction is normally caused by dirty ammunition/chamber or a pitted chamber due to lack of cleaning. If the rifle has a pitted chamber, it must be turned in to have the barrel replaced. This malfunction is a serious one since more complicated dexterity is needed to correct it and, of course, to do it quickly. Below is the breakdown of the corrective action to restore your rifle back to operation.

SYMPTOM - You are shooting a multiple-shot engagement and notice your bolt carrier did not go forward, you have a soft, mushy trigger, and it will not fire.

STEP ONE - Remove the magazine from the rifle.

STEP TWO - With your finger off the trigger, rotate the rifle to the right (ejection port down) and so you may still observe the ejection port. With the firing hand, rack the bolt carrier to the rear and continue to actuate it until the casing is cleared from the chamber. The worse case is that you will need to assemble your cleaning rod and punch this casing out while holding the bolt carrier to the rear.

STEP THREE - Rack the bolt to the rear at least three times to ensure the casing is extracted and ejected from the rifle. As you are doing this step, observe the casing being ejected and allow the slide to use its force to shut each time it is pulled to the rear.

STEP FOUR - Properly insert and seat a loaded magazine, listening to hear it click into the locked position, tug to ensure it is locked.

STEP FIVE - Rack the bolt fully to the rear and release it to close by its own spring tension. Your rifle is now ready to continue the engagement.

STEP SIX - Continue the engagement as the situation dictates.

NOTE: Correcting this malfunction needs to be practiced often since it is the most complicated to do under stress or when you lose dexterity because blood is leaving the extremities.

Appendix A - Ammunition

Special purpose 7.62x54R Cartridges
Over the years, a number of specialized cartridges have come into existence. In the early 1940s, special subsonic rounds were made for use in silenced weapons. These have two types of markings: one used before 1941 and the other used only after. We do not have any of these rounds to display here as they are very difficult to find. Another special round that was developed was the ranging incendiary or PZ cartridge. This round was developed for use in machine guns and is very dangerous to fire in infantry rifles. It has a complicated striker and explosive within the bullet. It is unstable and can explode if mishandled.

The last special-purpose cartridges that we know of were developed for use in the SVD sniper rifle and are known as the 7N1 and 7N14. These rounds were designed by Sabelnikov, Sazonov, and Dvoryaninov to be more accurate than the conventional ball ammunition then in service. According to Russian sources, the round proved to be 2.5 times more precise than the Type L or Type LPS in use at the time. It has no special markings and but can be distinguished from regular cartridges only by writing on the ammunition case.

Round Type	Picture/Color	Bullet Weight	Comments
M-91	Picture Not Available	13.636 grams (210 grains)	Early round nosed bullet, replaced in 1908. Brass cased with black powder loading.
Type D Heavy Ball (*Dal'noboinaya*)	Yellow Tip	182 grains	Discontinued in front line service by 1970.
Type LPS Light Ball (*Lyokhkaya Pulya Obrazets*)	Silver	148 grains	Is loaded with mild steel core.

Type L Light Ball (*Lyokhkaya Pulya Obrazets 1930*) Unmarked		148 grains	If made before 1970, this will be a lead-core bullet with copper plating. If made after 1969, it is loaded with a steel-core "LPS" bullet.
T-46 Tracer Green Tip		148 grains	The range of a tracer was required to be 1500 meters, but was actually closer to 1200 meters. The tracer compound was a mix of barium salts, magnesium, and aluminum.
BZT Armor Piercing Incendiary Tracer (*Broneboino-zazhitgatel'naya trassiruyushchaya*) Violet and Red Tip		142 grains (approx.)	Its burn compound was originally a phosphorous/aluminum mix; later rounds used thermite.
PZ Ranging Incendiary (*Pristrelnochno-zazhigatel'naya*) Red Tip		142 grains (approx)	Its burn compound was originally a phosphorous/aluminum mix; later rounds used thermite.
B-30 Armor Piercing (*Broneboinaya*) Black Tip		170 grains	
B-32 Armor Piercing-Incendiary (*Broneboino-zazhitgaltel'naya trassiruyushchaya*) Black & Red Tip		155 grains	Its burn compound was originally a phosphorous/aluminum mix; later rounds used thermite.

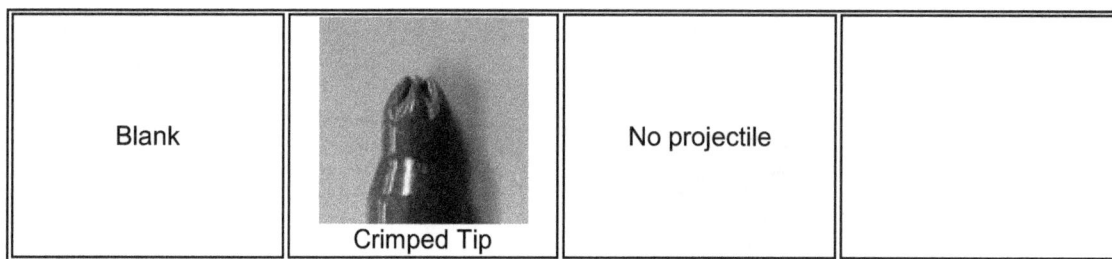

Blank	Crimped Tip	No projectile	

Figure C-1

Sources:

- *Soviet Small-Arms and Ammunition, by D.N. Bolotin, published by Finnish Arms Museum Foundation, 1995*

- *Military Small Arms of the 20th Century, 7th Edition, by Ian V. Hogg and John S. Weeks, published by Krause Publications, 2000*

- *The Mosin Nagant Rifle, by Terence W. Lapin, published by North Cape Publications, 1998*

- *AK-47 The Complete Kalashnikov Family of Assault Rifles, by Duncan Long, published by Paladin Press, Boulder, Colorado, 1988*

Appendix B - Ammunition Comparison

| 9x18mm Makarov | 9x19mm Luger | 7.62x25mm Tokarev | .45 ACP |

PISTOLS AND SUBMACHINE GUNS

Size Comparison of NATO vs. Non-Standard Ammunition

| 5.56x 45mm | 5.45x 39mm | 5.56x 45mm | 7.62x 39mm | 7.62x 51mm | 7.62x 54R mm | 12.7x 99mm | 12.7x 108mm |

ASSAULT RIFLES   **SNIPER RIFLES & MACHINE GUNS**

Appendix C - Non-Standard Ammunition Packaging & Markings

Packaging

Russian small arms cartridges are packed in sealed sheet-metal containers, with two containers per wooden crate. Older Russian production used rectangular containers of heavy gauge galvanized iron with soldered seams. Around 1959, the introduction of painted, rolled edge, rounded corner, tin plate 'sardine can' containers became the standard.

Metal and wooden crates have standardized markings that identify the contents as to caliber, functional type, cartridge case material, quantity and cartridge/powder lot data. Specialized cartridges are further identified by a color code consisting of one or two color stripes which correspond to bullet tip color. AP cartridges with tungsten carbide cores are identified by two concentric circles instead of color stripes. Russian cartridge designation, packaging and marking practices are generally followed by former Soviet-Bloc countries; each, however, has introduced some modifications in designation and marking. Russian ammunition packaging can be distinguished from Bulgarian packaging, which also carries Cyrillic markings, primarily by the different factory codes. The factory code on the container also appears in the headstamp of the cartridges in the container.

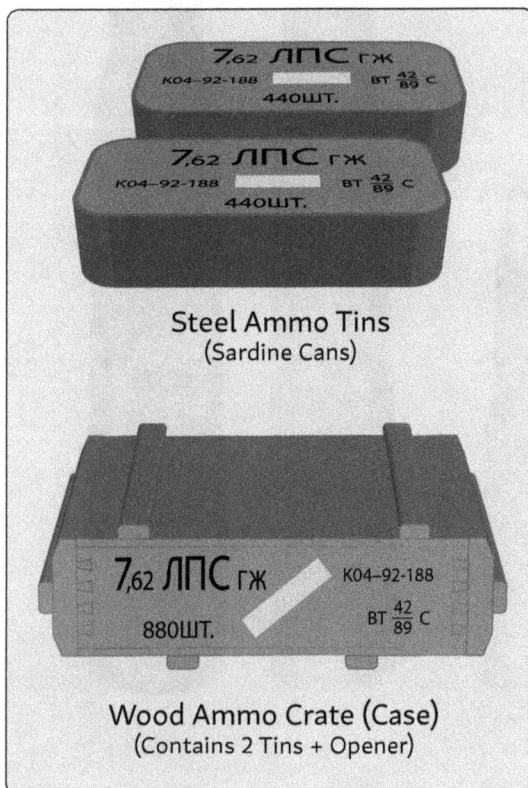

Steel Ammo Tins
(Sardine Cans)

Wood Ammo Crate (Case)
(Contains 2 Tins + Opener)

Cartridge quantities and weights of wooden crates

Country	Manufacturer	Caliber	Rounds /Crate	Crate Weight
Czech Rep.	Sellier and Bellot	14.5 x 114	210	53 kg.
India	OFB	14.5 x 114	60	15.5 kg.
Russia	Unknown	14.5 x 114	80	23 kg.
Bulgaria	Arsenal	12.7 x 108	200	29 kg.
Bulgaria	Arsenal	12.7 x 108	200	32 kg.
Pakistan	POF	12.7 x 108	280	42 kg.
Russia	Unknown	12.7 x 108	190	29 kg.
Russia	Novosibirsk	12.7 x 108	160	25 kg.
Bulgaria	Arsenal	7.62 x 54(R)	880	25 kg.
Czech Rep.	Sellier and Bellot	7.62 x 54(R)	800	24 kg.
Russia	Novosibirsk	7.62 x 54(R)	880	26 kg.
Russia	Novosibirsk	7.62 x 54(R)	600	21 kg.
Russia	Unknown	7.62 x 54(R)	880	26 kg.
Serbia	Prvi Partizan	7.62 x 54(R)	1,200	39 kg.
Czech Rep.	Sellier and Bellot	7.62 x 39	1,200	28 kg.
Pakistan	POF	7.62 x 39	1,750	39 kg.
Russia	Barnaul	7.62 x 39	1,320	30 kg.
Serbia	Prvi Partizan	7.62 x 39	1,260	29 kg.
Sudan	STC	7.62 x 39	1,500	28.1 kg.
Ukraine	Lugansk	7.62 x 39	1,320	30 kg.
Yugoslavia	Igman Zavod	7.62 x 39	1,260	28 kg.
Yugoslavia	Igman Zavod	7.62 x 39	1,120	27.5 kg.
Russia	Unknown	5.45 x 39	2,160	29 kg.
Ukraine	Lugansk	5.45 x 39	2,160	29 kg.

Non-Standard Ammunition tin and crate marking - diagrams

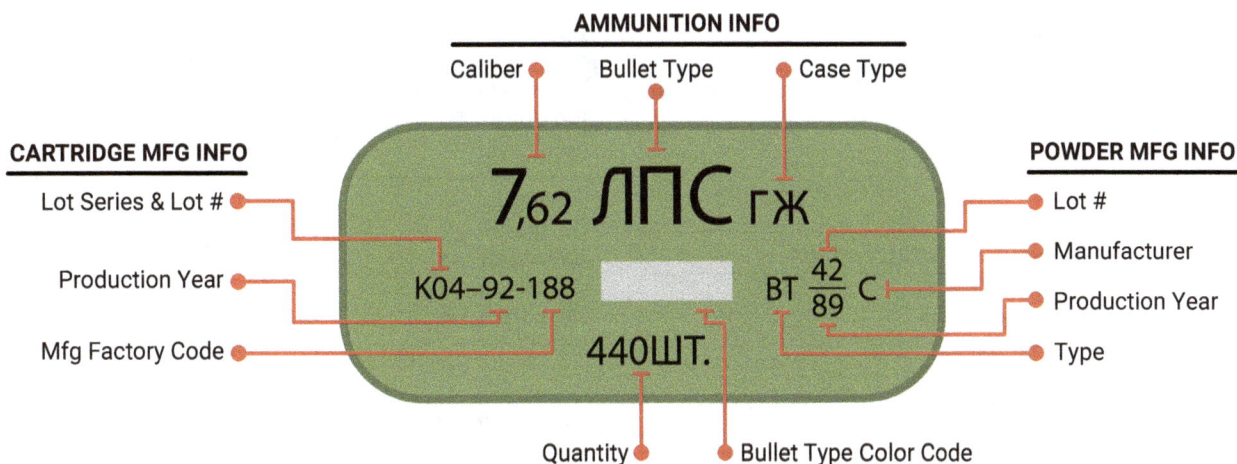

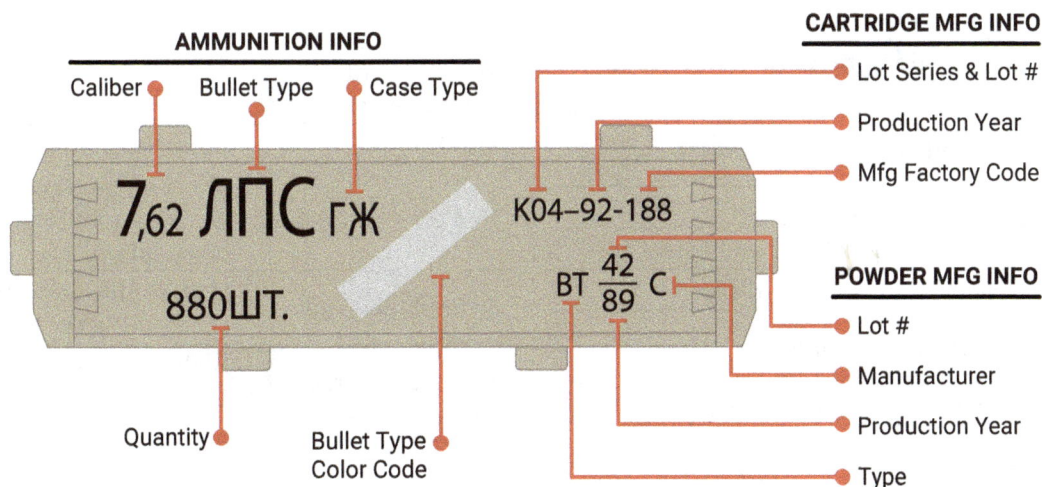

AMMUNITION INFO

Caliber · Bullet Type · Case Type

CARTRIDGE MFG INFO

Lot Series & Lot #

Production Year

Mfg Factory Code

POWDER MFG INFO

Lot #

Manufacturer

Production Year

Type

7,62 ЛПС ГЖ

К04–92–188

BT $\frac{42}{89}$ C

440ШТ.

Quantity · Bullet Type Color Code

AMMUNITION INFO

Caliber · Bullet Type · Case Type

CARTRIDGE MFG INFO

Lot Series & Lot #

Production Year

Mfg Factory Code

POWDER MFG INFO

Lot #

Manufacturer

Production Year

Type

7,62 ЛПС ГЖ

880ШТ.

К04–92–188

BT $\frac{42}{89}$ C

Quantity

Bullet Type Color Code

Non-Standard Ammunition tin and crate marking - Russian ammunition data

CASE TYPE MARKINGS

Mark	Meaning
ГЖ	Bimetallic case (gilding metal clad steel)
ГЛ	Brass case
ГС	Steel case

CARTRIDGE MFG FACTORY CODES

Code	Location
3	Ulyanovsk
17	Barnaul
38	Yuryuzan
60	Frunze (now Bishkek)
188	Novosibirsk
270	Voroshilovgrad (now Luhansk)
304	Lugansk
539	Tula
711	Klimovsk
T	Tula

Non-Standard Ammunition tin and crate marking - Russian ammunition data

BULLET TYPE MARKINGS

Mark	Meaning
Б Б-30 Б-32 БП	Armor-piercing
Б3	Armor-piercing incendiary
Б3Т Б3Т-44	Armor-piercing incendiary tracer
БС БС-40 БС-41	Armor-piercing with special core of tungsten carbide instead of carbon steel
БСТ	Armor-piercing with tungsten carbide core with added tracer
БТ	Armor-piercing tracer
Д	Heavy (long-range) with lead core instead of carbon steel
З ЗП	Incendiary
Л	Lightweight bullet
ЛПС	Light ball bullet with mild steel core
МДЗ	High explosive incendiary
П П-41	Spotting / ranging
ПЗ	Incendiary spotting / ranging
ПП	Enhanced penetration
ПС	Spotting / ranging with mild steel core
ПТ	Spotting / ranging tracer
СНБ	Armor-piercing sniper
Т Т-30 Т-45 Т-46	Tracer
57-У-322 57-У-323	Cartridge with higher powder charge
57-У-423	High-pressure cartridge
57-Х-322 57-Х-323 57-Х-340	Blank cartridge
57-НЕ-УЧ	Training cartridge
7Н1	Sniper bullet

BULLET TYPE COLOR CODES (Ammunition up to 14.5mm)

Color	Meaning
No color	Ball
White tip	Reference Ball
Silver tip	Light ball with steel core
Yellow tip	Heavy ball, or ball with torpedo base (on 7.62x54R)
Blue tip + white band	Short range ball 14.5x114 (only Hungarian and Czech)
Green tip + white band	Short range, tracer, (only Czech designation, only found on 7.62x39 with round nose)
Green tip	Tracer
Green tip & head-stamp or entire cartridge green	Subsonic ammunition for silencer-weapons
Red tip	Spotting charge, incendiary
Red tip + white band	Short range tracer ball 14.5x114 (only Hungarian designation)
Entire bullet red	High explosive bullet (7.62x54R after 1945)
Entire bullet red	High explosive bullet (on 12.7 and 14.5mm)
Magenta tip + red band	Armor piercing incendiary tracer
Black tip + red band	Armor piercing incendiary
Black tip + red shell	Armor piercing incendiary with tungsten carbide core
Black tip + yellow band	Armor piercing incendiary Phosphorus 12.7
Black tip	Armor piercing

** The bullet tip color codes in the table above will be the same color codes on the tins or crates, but they will be color stripes on the packaging.

Example:

CARTRIDGE
Black Tip + Red Band

TIN or CRATE
Black Stripe + Red Stripe

Appendix D - Non-Standard Weapon Identification Markings

General Identification Markings

There are various identification markings found on non-standard weapons. Typically the markings will provide some or all of the following information:
- factory name or stamp (proof mark)
- caliber & serial number
- selector lever markings/symbols
- rear sight mark/symbol

NOTE: Data tables are not all inclusive, but they cover the more common weapon manufacturers.

Selector Lever Markings on Kalashnikov Rifles

Upper/ Safe Symbol	Mid/ Full-Auto Symbol	Lower/ Semi-Auto Symbol	Country
	Д	1	Albania
	L	D	Albania
	AB	ЕД	Bulgaria
	L	D	China
	进	单	China
	30	1	Czechoslovakia
	آ	رى	Egypt
	D	E	Egypt
	D	E	East Germany
	∞	1	Hungary
آ	ص	م	Iraq
	련	다	North Korea
	C	P	Poland
	Z	O	Poland
S	A	R	Romania
S	FA	FF	Romania
	1	3	Romania
	ЛР	ОГОНЬ	Russia
	АВ	ОД	Russia
U	R	ᴊ	Yugo/Serbia

Rear Sight Marks on Kalashnikov Rifles

Symbol	Country
D	Albania
П	Bulgaria
D	China
N	East Germany
A	Hungary
П	North Korea
S	Poland
P	Romania
П	Russia
O	Yugo/Serbia

Non-Standard Weapon Identification Markings

Factory Stamps and Countries of Manufacture

The table of symbols below are factory stamps (proof marks) for non-standard weapons. The symbols will identify the country of manufacture of the weapon. NOTE: *This is not an all inclusive list, but it covers the more common weapon manufacturers.*

(10) Bulgaria	(21) Bulgaria	(25) Bulgaria	△ China
(386) China	△36 China	△66 China	△ China
Egypt	East Germany	(3) East Germany	(K3) East Germany
East Germany	(06) East Germany	Iraq	Iraq
☆ North Korea	★ North Korea	(11) Poland	Romania
Russia	Russia	Russia	Russia
☆ Russia	Russia	Russia	Russia
Ⓩ Yugoslavia/Serbia	**M.70.AB2** Yugoslavia/Serbia	ZASTAVA-KRAGUJEVAC Yugoslavia/Serbia	

Appendix E - Non-standard weapons theory overview

There are three key concepts to understand when manipulating non-standard weapons. These simple and logical concepts are:

1. **CYCLE OF OPERATIONS**
2. **OPERATING SYSTEMS**
3. **LOCKING SYSTEMS**

> Firearm design trends are shared across region, manufacturer and class of weapon and are relatively obvious to recognize.
>
> Keep in mind that firearms are essentially simple machines that harness the energy created by the fired cartridge to operate the system.

CYCLE OF OPERATIONS (COO)

The cycle of operations is a crucial basis for understanding how the weapon operates and for function/malfunction diagnosis. Each specific malfunction will correspond to a specific step or sometimes two in the COO. A failure in the system at a certain point, will by default, cause a failure of omission of all subsequent steps. (example – a failure to properly extract will manifest as a failure to eject.)

The COO will vary based on the type of operating and locking systems. Once the operating and locking systems of the weapon are known, the COO is logical.

The examples below all start from a standard reference point: the weapon is loaded, charged, placed on fire and the trigger is pulled.

'Cycle of Operations' Examples:

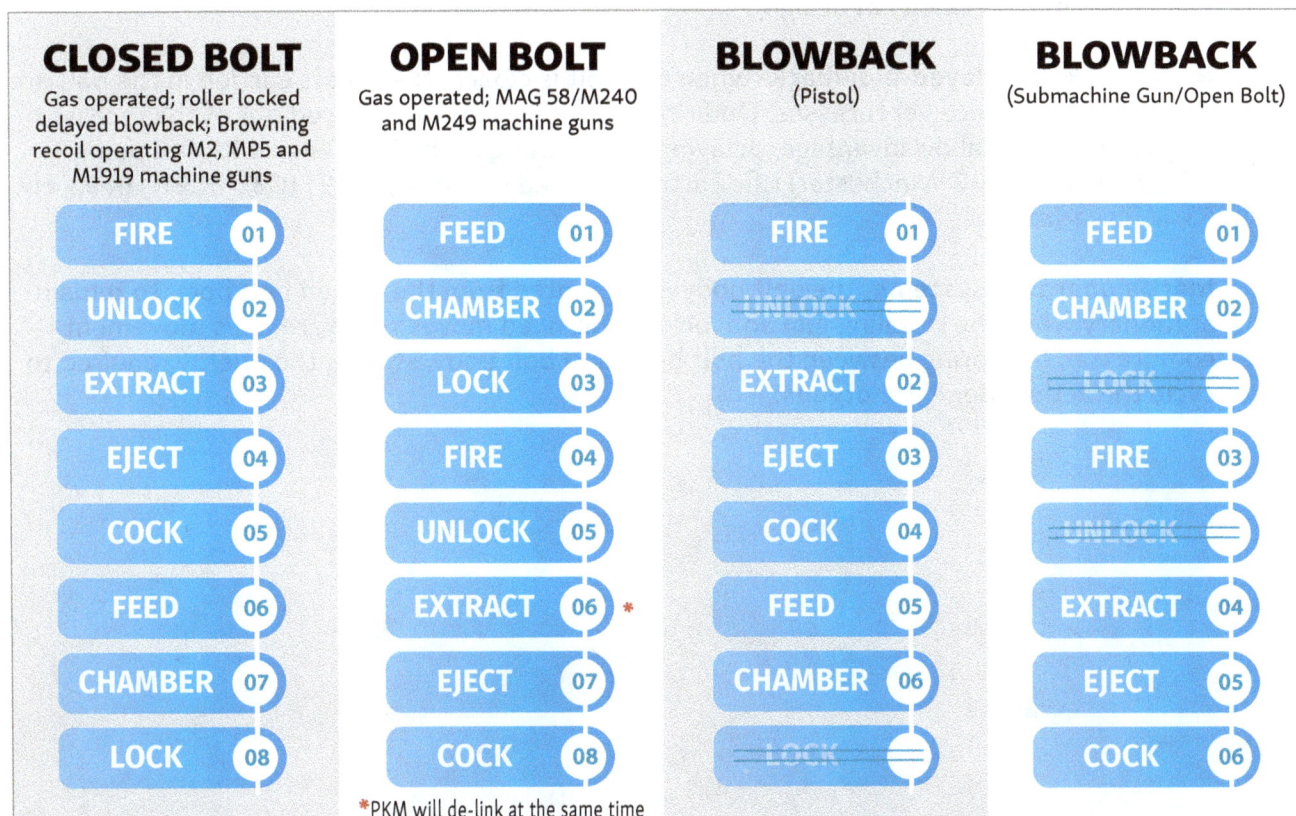

CLOSED BOLT	OPEN BOLT	BLOWBACK	BLOWBACK
Gas operated; roller locked delayed blowback; Browning recoil operating M2, MP5 and M1919 machine guns	Gas operated; MAG 58/M240 and M249 machine guns	(Pistol)	(Submachine Gun/Open Bolt)
FIRE 01	FEED 01	FIRE 01	FEED 01
UNLOCK 02	CHAMBER 02	~~UNLOCK~~	CHAMBER 02
EXTRACT 03	LOCK 03	EXTRACT 02	~~LOCK~~
EJECT 04	FIRE 04	EJECT 03	FIRE 03
COCK 05	UNLOCK 05	COCK 04	~~UNLOCK~~
FEED 06	EXTRACT 06 *	FEED 05	EXTRACT 04
CHAMBER 07	EJECT 07	CHAMBER 06	EJECT 05
LOCK 08	COCK 08	~~LOCK~~	COCK 06

*PKM will de-link at the same time

Non-standard weapons theory overview *(continued ...)*

⚙ OPERATING SYSTEMS

1. **Direct Impingement**- a type of gas operation that directs gas from a fired cartridge directly to the bolt carrier or slide assembly to cycle the action. (AR-15/M4 variants)

2. **Long-stroke piston system**- the piston is mechanically fixed to the bolt group and moves through the entire operating cycle. (AK variants)

3. **Short-stroke piston system (tappet system)**- the piston moves separately from the bolt group. It may directly push the bolt group parts as n the M1 carbine or operate through a connecting rod. (HK 416, AR180, POF, LWRC, FN FAL)

4. **Blowback**- the system of operation for self-loading firearms that obtains energy from the motion of the cartridge case as it is pushed to the rear by expanding gases created by the ignition of the propellant charge. (STEN, Makarov, M3 Grease Gun)

5. **Short recoil action**- the barrel and slide recoil only a short distance before they unlock and separate. The barrel stops quickly, and the slide continues rearward compressing the recoil spring and performing extraction, ejection and finally feeding a fresh round from the magazine in the counter recoil phase. During the last portion of its forward travel, the slide locks into the barrel and pushes the barrel back into battery. *(This is found in most handguns chambered for 9x19mm Parabellum or greater caliber. Smaller calibers, 9x18mm Makarov and below, generally use the blowback method of operation due to lower chamber pressure and associated simplicity of design.)

6. **Roller-locked, delayed-blowback**- when the bolt is closed, the rollers carried in the bolt are wedged into the receiver recesses. On firing, the rollers must be forced out of the recesses at great mechanical disadvantage, delaying the opening of the bolt, even with full power 7.62mm NATO (.308 Winchester) rifle cartridges used in the G3/HK 91 (G3, HK 91, HK 93, HK 53, MP5 variants)

7. **Inertia operated systems**- the bolt body is separated from the locked bolt body to remain stationary while the recoiling gun and locked bolt head moves rearward. This movement compresses the spring between the bolt head and bolt body, storing the energy required to cycle the action. Benelli shotguns.

Non-standard weapons theory overview *(continued ...)*

🔒 **LOCKING SYSTEMS**

1. **None** - all blowback pistols and some submachine guns – (STEN, UZI, M3 Grease Gun, Makarov, and CZ 82)

2. **Roller** - (HK variants, MG3, MG34, MG 42 and CZ 52)

3. **Rotating bolt** - (AK, Stoner, M60, and M249)

4. **Tilting bolt** - (SKS, FN FAL and MAG 58/M240)

5. **Tilting barrel** - (Tokarev TT33, Sig variants, M1911 variants and Glock variants)

6. **Rotating barrel** - (MAB P15, Colt All American 2000, and Beretta 8000)

7. **Locking flaps** - (RPD, DP/DPM and DShK)

8. **Falling locking block** - (P38, M9, and VZ58)

Function check

Checking the mechanical function of a weapon by replicating, without ammunition, the firing modes from the lowest rate of fire (SAFE if applicable) to the highest in a progressive sequence (not by selector location). The parts checked are the safety/safeties, sear and disconnector.

M4A1
1. Ensure the rifle is clear
2. Charge and place the weapon on SAFE
3. Attempt to fire (weapons should not FIRE, safety is functioning)
4. Place the weapon on SEMI, pull the trigger and hold it to the rear (hammer should fall, trigger/sear functioning)
5. Maintain the trigger to the rear and cycle the bolt
6. Release the trigger and listen for a metallic click (disconnector functioning)
7. Pull the trigger again and the hammer should fall
8. Charge the weapon and place on AUTO
9. Pull the trigger and hold it to the rear then cycle the bolt more than once
10. Release the trigger and pull it again, nothing should happen (auto sear is functioning)
11. Charge the weapon then pull the trigger again and the hammer should fall
12. Function check complete

Significant visual indicators
- Any checked, knurled or serrated surface
- Any movable lever or switch
- Pins with gripping surfaces
- Index marks (two lines that need to be aligned to disassembled (CZ 75)
- Recoil spring with ends of different diameters

---

www.ingramcontent.com/pod-product-compliance
Lightning Source LLC
Chambersburg PA
CBHW080526110426
42742CB00017B/3251